MUSIC INDUSTRY CONNECTION

THE TRUTH ABOUT
Record Pools & Music Conferences
Talent Shows & Open-Mics

by
JAWAR

1

Copyright 2006 Music Industry Connection, LLC
ISBN: 0-9759380-2-9
Library of Congress Control Number

by JaWar

FIRST EDITION

Published by

Music Industry Connection, LLC
P.O. Box 52682, Atlanta, GA 30355, USA
800-963-0949 www.mt101.com questions@mt101.com

Printed in the U.S.A.

The information provided in this book is intended only as a resource guide for record companies, aspiring artists, producers, djs, talent showcase & open mic organizers, managers and other professionals in the business of music. Remember to always verify the company and contact names found in this book before submitting material. There are a number of resources needed to achieve success in the business of music that are not contained in this book. The authors and publishers have attempted to verify the accuracy of the resources in this book; however, the information provided is subject to change. The authors and publisher disclaim all responsibility for any loss or damages from dealing with the companies mention in this book. Always seek the guidance and advice of qualified music business professionals.

Cover Design: **Ashil at Design Apart**
Edited by: **Seneferu Ast**

My goal is to provide the most comprehensive directory of United States Music Conferences and Record Pools that may be used by artists, producers, managers, entertainment attorneys, website designers, graphic artists, accountants, certified public accountants, record pools, DJs, songwriters, music publishers, music publicists, distribution companies, music consultants, music magazines, music organizations, record stores, radio stations, record companies, recording studios, distributors, musicians, talent show & open mic organizers and other music industry professionals to help them achieve their goals and realize their potential within the shortest time frame possible while providing the highest quality service.

In addition, the book is designed to give aspiring artists, producers and managers practical steps and tips for achieving success while attending a music conference, talent showcase, open-mic or servicing a record pool. Remember to always verify your information and the companies you intend on doing business with. This book is merely a directory and resource guide and does not constitute an endorsement of the companies contained herein.

AC-KNOW-LEDGE-MENTS

I want to thank the Creator and the Ancestors for giving me another opportunity to make a positive difference in someone else's life. As a traveling man I have met a number of people who have purchased one of my other books under the Music Industry Connection Book Series and/or have attended a Music Therapy 101 Conference, Seminar or Workshop Series. Thank you for your continue investment and support.

DEDICATIONS

This book is dedicated to the talent showcase organizers who have an issue with me networking and promoting the *Atlanta Music Industry Connection Book* at their event simply because "every time they see me I am networking and promoting the *Atlanta Music Industry Connection Book.*" This book is dedicated to the industry professionals who have never attended a free Music Therapy 101 Workshop at the Public Library, but have asked to be a featured speaker at one. This book is dedicated to the industry professionals who gave their word they would speak at a free Music Therapy 101 Music Business Workshop at the Public Library, but did a no call, no show. This book is dedicated to the artists who only want to perform at a music conference and not attend the informative panels, workshops and seminars provided. This book is dedicated to the good folks who hoped, prayed and thought I would only write and release the *Atlanta Music Industry Connection Book*. This book is dedicated to the bookstore that would not sell the *Atlanta Music Industry Connection Book* and would not give me the reason why, while they were selling a number of other music business book titles. This book is dedicated to the record store that stopped selling the *Atlanta Music Industry Connection Book*, but what not give a reason why. This book is dedicated to the myth that if you want to hide something from a group of people you put it in a book that is a **horrible myth** that we need to abolish, today. This book is dedicated to the industry types that I know personally that do not want me at their event, but don't have the balls to tell me why. This book is dedicated to people who always attempt to financially low-ball me although their businesses have generated thousands of dollars from being in the *Atlanta Music Industry Connection Book* for free. This book is dedicated to music business professionals who tell music industry insiders not to do business with me, but can't give an ethical reason why.

TABLE OF CONTENTS

MUSIC CONFERENCES

RECORD POOLS

TALENT SHOWS & OPEN-MICS

MUSIC CONFERENCES

When should I go to a music conference?

Attend music conferences when you want to network with industry professionals and learn about the inner workings of the business of music. Both newcomers and industry veterans alike benefit from attending music conferences.

What should I expect from music conferences?

You should expect to have fun, increase your industry contacts and learn new and existing trends related to the music business. In addition, expect for the organizers of the music conference to deliver what they said they were going to deliver.

Can I get signed from performing at a music conference?

While the exception is that you may get signed from performing at a music conference the rule is that you will not. Use your music conference experience to further your knowledge on the business of music, increase your industry contacts and improve your stage performance and you will get much more from the conference than attempting to get signed. You should also invite local print media and promoters to your showcase, as this may lead to music reviews, interviews and possible paying gigs (shows).

Differences between a Music Conference, Workshop, Seminar and Panel Discussion

A music conference normally encompasses workshops, seminars and panel discussions and tends to be either all-day or over several days. By design conferences are typically dynamic in scope offering the attendee and those involved with a number of networking and educational opportunities. Seminars tend be in lecture format, they generally last no more than one to three hours and are often held by one person. Workshops on the other hand offer attendees the opportunity to interact with the speaker or speakers. Workshops, by design, have a classroom feel, often providing handouts, lecture notes and power point or overhead projector displays. I have seen workshops last anywhere from one hour to all day. Panel discussions generally have between three to seven people. The people often come from various backgrounds within the same industry. For instance, there may be a panel discussion on "Breaking into the Music Biz", however, the panelists may include a music producer, entertainment attorney, music manager, booking agent, recording engineer, publicist and DJ. To contact Music Therapy 101 National Music Conference about scheduling a workshop, seminar or panel discussion in your city call 800-963-0949.

What does it cost to attend a music conference?

I have seen registration prices for music conferences vary from free to $999. Most conferences offer reduced rates for early registration; take advantage of this and save money. In addition, when traveling you will incur a number of other expenses outlined below.

Being resourceful can save you a great deal of money. For instance, you may ask friends, family and business associates if they know anyone who works for an airline that may be willing to give you their buddy or companion pass. Buddy passes are issued by airlines to their employees. However, be mindful that buddy-passes are stand by tickets, meaning that your seat is not guaranteed until the plane is in the air. Once, I waited nearly 24 hours at the airport before being able to get on the plane while using a buddy pass. If you do purchase your ticket out right remember that getting it at least two weeks in advance will ensure a lower rate.

While it is normally a good idea to lodge at the host hotel where the conference is being held it may not always be financially feasible. When your budget does not allow for you to lodge at the host hotel, attempt to stay with relatives, old college friends and members of your fraternity or sorority, etc. Also, you may find other musicians, producers, artists, managers, etc. in your town that are going to the conference and that would be willing to split the room rate with you. However, be mindful of different lifestyle habits. For instance, you would not want to room with someone who smokes if you did not or vice versa.

In addition, use the Internet to find discounts on room rates. Hotels.com normally offers discounted room rates. Always ask if you would receive discounts by being an AAA Member or by using a certain credit card. Remember you won't know until you ask.

Some of your expenses may include conference registration price, performance fee, lodging/hotel, air fare, train fare, rental car, fuel cost, food, and/or promotional material: business cards-flyers-CDs, taxes and miscellaneous items.

Reduce the cost of going to a music conference.

- Volunteer
- Bartering Services
- Student Registration
- Early Registration

Some music conferences allow for complimentary registration to volunteers. Usually, volunteering details may be found on the conference's website. If you don't see any details, always email or call about volunteering opportunities. In addition to volunteering, you may be able to offer bartering services to the conference. For instance, you may offer to promote the conference through your growing ezine, print publication or website. Furthermore, you may offer to distribute flyers at talent shows, open-mics and music business networking events in exchange for a complimentary pass to the conference. Many conferences have student and early-bird registration discounts. Now that you have the most comprehensive list of United States Music Conferences you should be able to get the early bird registration on future music conferences.

When should I stop going to music conferences?

Over the pass 10 years the music industry has witnessed tremendous change in the production, marketing, distribution and royalty collection of intellectual properties. Many of the changes are discussed at various music conferences throughout the year. In addition, every music conference will offer you the opportunity to network with new professionals and strengthen ties with familiar ones. Going to music conferences also offers you the ability to brand yourself and company to other industry professionals. Whenever possible, you will want to attend a music conference.

How many conferences should I attend?

You should attend as many conferences as it takes for you to accomplish your goal. Your goals should be very specific and doable. When I attend a music conference my very specific goals are to sell one of my books to everyone at the conference, to distribute my flyers to everyone at the conference and to collect a business card, flyer or email address from everyone I meet. I attempt to attend or at least have a presence at every music conference that is held in Atlanta, since this is where I reside. In addition, I attempt to attend two new music conferences a year.

How do I know if a conference is legit?

Before attending any music conference write down your goals. You should have three to five specific goals that are no longer than two sentences. By having specific goals you ensure that you get your money's worth and that the conference is legit.

With that said, you will want to find out how long the conference has been in business and ask fellow musicians if they have attended the conference and if their expectations were met and/or exceeded. Visit the conference website and read how many details are given. For instance, there should be details on the speakers, panels and workshops. Normally, I will have heard and/or seen advertising from a legit conference through a number of different sources. These sources may include print and on-line media, e-blast, radio and word-of-mouth. Go with your instinct. If you think it will be legit it probably is, however, if it seems too good to be true then it probably is.

Preparing for a music conference

You should get the conference directory and contact all of the attendees prior to going to the conference whenever possible. Write down three to five specific goals you want to accomplish while attending the conference.

A few of my goals while attending any music conference are to sell as many books as possible, more specifically to generate enough money to cover my travel expenses, to distribute the Music Industry Connection & Music Therapy 101 flyers to everyone in attendance and to get everyone's contact information that may come in the form of a business card, flyer, CD or by having new contacts complete a short form. By having these specific goals, I know that I need to have enough inventory before attending a conference. I need books, flyers and paper to ensure my goals can be met. As an artist, producer, manager, publicists or promoter you may need to order CDs, flyers, business cards and press kits before attending any conference. If it normally takes you five days to get your promotional CDs or business cards, put in an order 10 to 15 days prior to the conference. This will ensure that you have some cushion time. Remember you have no control over your manufactures equipment failure and acts of GOD. However, you do have control over how you use your time with precision planning and preparation. I found that in planning for the unexpected, time is one of our most valuable assets.

What should I do while at a music conference?

Network with everyone at the conference- you never know who is going to change your life forever. Keep smiling and have fun! The conference is an experience that may yield you great rewards. Get as many business cards, flyers and promotional CDs as possible. Listen to what others are saying. You will learn something new even if it is merely someone's new perspective on an old issue.

What to do after attending a music conference?

You should take a shower or long bath, brush your teeth and relax. Music conferences can be quite exhausting when you are truly networking.

After you have gotten your bearings, you will want to add your new contacts into your music business database(s). Then, you will want to contact via phone or email those contacts that seem to be most promising for your career and business. Next, you will want to send a thank you note to everyone who you met, reemphasizing who you are, what you do and how your services may benefit them. For instance, you would write:

> I am JaWar, a songwriter and recording artist who is available for co-writing opportunities. In addition, I have thirty original hip hop, jazz, pop and gospel songs, recorded, mixed and mastered that are available for movie soundtracks, commercial jingles, ringtones and other licensing formats. You may reach me at either jawar@mt101.com or 800-963-0949 to discuss details about licensing these original sound recordings.

How should I dress at music conferences?

Dress in what makes you most comfortable and that which allows you to brand your image. Keep in mind that you never know who you are going to meet at a music conference. Special guest show up at music conferences all the time- especially the more established ones.

This may seem like a "no-brainer", but bring some breath mints with you. What a tragedy it would be if the person you were talking to had one thing on their mind: getting as far away from *you* as possible because your breath wreaks of something awful. While music conferences tend to be a business/social environment, it may be a great idea to not drink until the evening hours. The worse is to walk into a 10AM Panel Discussion smelling like the party already got started.

Why do I need mints at a music conference?

I attended a music conference and was talking with an extremely intelligent, attractive woman. She was very polite and professional, unfortunately I was not able to focus on what she was saying because her breath smelled awful. Word to the wise: always have a few breath mints and/or gum handy. Normally, mints may be found throughout the host hotel where the conference is being held.

How to make real connections at a conference?

Before you can *make* a real connection at a conference you must be able to *identify* a real connection. A real connection is anyone that will help you achieve your goal and realize your success. Real connections may be made anytime during your music conference experience. For instance, you may meet someone in the restroom, hotel lobby, during a panel discussion, in the hotel parking lot and during the showcases.

Many of my connections are made while walking to and from the host hotel to my car. Remember a music conference affords you a rare opportunity to meet a number of industry newcomers and seasoned veterans alike. Network at all times during the conference. If there is a time you should not sleep- a music conference is it.

Real Networking

While more established, heavily promoted conferences tend to be well attended, often you can get some of your best networking accomplished at smaller local music panel discussions, workshops, seminars and conferences like Music Therapy 101. However, it is important to always write down your goals and objectives, as this will help you maximize your experience. During a smaller conference, the setting tends to be a lot more intimate giving attendees and panelists the opportunity to get to know each other better and get beyond the small talk. Meaning you get past talking about where a person is from, why the came to the conference and their involvement in the music industry to how you can create a mutually beneficial arrangement that would allow both your companies to grow and generate more revenue (money). Given that both parties have a proven system, know how they can help someone else and how they can be helped, contracts may be signed before leaving the conference and that is real networking.

As a note you will always want to have a competent entertainment attorney draft and review any contracts you sign. Both parties should have legal representation before signing an agreement. You will find a list of competent entertainment attorneys in the Atlanta Music Industry Connection & Los Angeles Music Industry Connection Books. Ordering details may be found at the end of this book or by visiting www.mt101.com.

Should I go solo or with a crew to a conference?

Only take essential personnel to a music conference. Remember everyone has to get to the conference, eat and have a place to sleep. The more people you bring, the more money it will cost you. Keep in mind that attending a music conference is a business trip where your company incurs business expenses. As such, some (if not all) of your expenses are tax deductible. Keep all of your receipts related to attending a music conference. However, you will want to speak with your professional tax consultant or C.P.A. (Certified Public Accountant), as I do not provide business tax consulting services.

Which panels should I attend?

Given that there may be several panels being held at the same time, you will want to go to the panels that most relate to accomplishing your goals and realizing your success. In addition, depending on your knowledge base on the business of music, you will want to attend panels discussing copyrights, trademarks, publishing, new media, marketing and other legal issues. Unfortunately, it seems to be very consistent at music conferences that the super music producer or A&R panels are filled to capacity, but during the new media and technology panels there are very few people in them. The new media and technology panels are where independents should flock as this is where they can learn how to maximize their branding and marketing efforts for a fraction of the cost and with minimum effort.

When does the networking begin?

Networking for the conference could start as soon as you register. For instance, some music conferences offer the contact names, phone numbers and email addresses of attendees. With this list you could begin contacting those professionals who may help you achieve your goals and realize you're potential.

It was about 10:30 am and I noticed a young woman sitting next to a stack of a relatively new music magazine. I asked the young lady what she did and if she minded if I sat next to her. She mentioned that she was the publicist for the new magazine and that it was OK to sit. After about thirty minutes of networking the young lady said that she was preparing to leave because nothing was going on with the conference. I informed her that the panel discussions for the conference did not start until twelve noon. In addition, I asked the young lady to look around us and tell me what she saw. She said that she saw a few people. I told her that I saw opportunity. "You see" I said, "The people in the hotel lobby and walking around are probably from out of town and came to attend the conference. In addition, the persons probably have already had breakfast and are looking for something to do." This, I told her, was one of the best times to network, because the people had nothing to do and nowhere to go.

Making contacts at music conferences is equally, if not more important, than attending panel discussions at the conference. Networking should be employed throughout your entire visit at the conference. You never know whom you will meet and how that person may impact your life and music career. Always look to create opportunities by networking with as many people as you can while attending the conference.

How do I network at a conference?

Always have business cards or flyers with you while at a music conference. Typically, I distribute my fliers to everyone in the host conference hotel, as it is not always easy to identify who is there for the conference. By giving out flyers or business cards to everyone, you accomplish a couple goals. First, you easily promote yourself to other industry professionals. Second, you create windows of opportunity for yourself. If someone is interested in what your flyer reads or how it looks, they may immediately begin asking you questions about your involvement in the music business. At this point, you have just made a contact and networking has begun.

The conferences showcases and after parties are also great places to network. During these events people tend to be very relaxed, receptive and open for conversation. Generally, I move about the showcase hall or club handing out business cards while introducing myself. In addition, you may begin your networking while greeting someone that you already know and ask them to introduce you to someone new. This is one of the best ways to break the ice with a new contact as it gives you a form of credibility.

If you are speaking with someone and the conversations seems a bit dry or the person does not seem very interested, you may want to move on. With so many people attending a music conference you want to reach as many as possible. Don't take it personal if the person is not as excited as you are. There may be a number of reasons that they are not actively involved in the conversation. They could be nervous as all break out, have just received a whim of bad news, may not understand what the hell you're talking about or in my case be hungry!

Why brand myself & company at a conference?

The best artists, singers, songwriters and producers are not always the ones that rise to the crème of the crop. Rather, it is the ones that constantly work on improving their skills and brand themselves to industry professionals and the buying public that create greater opportunities for success.

I meet a number of people while attending conferences; however, the ones that I tend to do business with are the ones that I have come to know over time. These generally are the companies that place ads in print and on-line media, distribute flyers, send e-blast and constantly bring awareness to their company. Most music business books have a chapter or section dedicated to branding, marketing or promotions. Remember to read these sections, as the information is normally very helpful. Also, it may spark your creative juices. Ensure that you increase your knowledge base, so that you can maximize your branding potential at conferences. Read all that you can and learn from the experience, knowledge and wisdom of others.

What to know about the local music scene

While there are many professionals you will want to know in any particular market, I have identified a couple that may be keep in helping your music conference experience be worth the investment. Generally, you may find the professionals below on the Internet and from books such as the Atlanta Music Industry Connection or the Los Angeles Music Industry Connection by JaWar. Ordering details for these books may be found at the end of this book or at www.mt101.com

🎧 **MUSIC RETAIL STORES**

> ✓ You will want to know where all of the music retail stores are located. This would include

major chains and independents as well. Typically, independent stores allow you to post flyers. You will also get a pulse for what the local scene is like by gathering flyers from local artist and promoters. You have a greater opportunity of getting your music placed in a local store than you do with a major chain, so it would be wise to ask who the owner, manager or person responsible for putting new music in the store is.

ω PRINT AND ONLINE MEDIA

✓ You will want to find the local music and entertainment magazines and who is responsible for reviewing new music and interviewing artist. Getting these details prior to attending a conference or talent show would be great as you could invite the music editor to see you perform in an effort to get your music reviewed.

ω CLUBS, VENUES & PLACES TO PLAY

✓ Knowing the clubs and venues that cater to your style of music in any particular area may be extremely beneficial. By having this information you could set up a show where you could perform on a return visit to the city. You would use your attendance at the music conference as a way to promote your performance in the local market at a later date.

ω COLLEGES & UNIVERSITIES

✓ There is typically some population of the college audience that listens to your style of music. The goal is to reach that population and promote relentlessly to them. This may be done through a number of ways including distributing flyers, having your music played on the college radio station, getting a feature in the college newspaper, playing live and having a presence on popular sites such as mypsace.com, etc.

◉ PROMOTERS

✓ Local club, street, radio and concert promoters for your style of music can be instrumental in helping you understand the landscape for their market. Often they can tell you who the go-to-people are in the city. They also tend to have an extensive contact list of industry professionals that can help make breaking into the local market a lot easier. Local promoters typically have some presence at national conferences in their own backyard as they are seeking new clients.

◉ PUBLICISTS

✓ Publicists tend to be a fun group to network with. More importantly, they may be key players in helping you get a great deal of exposure through media channels, such as newspapers, magazines, radio, the internet and T.V. I have met a number of people who claim to be publicists, but don't do much more than distribute your flyers. While there is nothing wrong with distributing flyers, this is not truly publicity. A publicist will know the key people in media who can give an artist, producer, label or band additional exposure. Hiring a publicist prior to performing at a music conference may help you secure media exposure through print and online media.

✓ Radio has its place for promoting artist. However, I am not that big on it, as I think for most independent artist commercial radio is overrated. The reality is that it normally takes an abundance of financial and human resources to truly make radio work for you. College and non-commercial radio stations are ideal for independent artist seeking to get on-air interviews and music played.

Can I really get laid at a music conference?

I have never had any luck; however, if your experience is any different please share your story by emailing me at jawar@mt101.com. Remember to protect yourself, keep your moral/spiritual/religious values intact and last, but not least, what happens on the road stays on the road!

How do I know if my trip was a success?

Your measuring stick as to if your music conference experience was a success will be directly related to how many of your goals you were able to accomplish. Your goals should be clearly identifiable and put in writing. Truth be told, it may be weeks, months, even years before you really get the full impact of attending a music conference.

Every conference you attend should be viewed as yet another opportunity to plant seeds; and like the natural order of things it may take until the next season (year) before those seeds sprout. It may take even more seasons (years) before the seed is able to bear fruit from which you may eat. With that being said, remember to plant many seeds (attend many conferences) and your trips are bound to be a success.

How do I organize a music conference?

Organizing a successful music conference requires vision, practical planning, execution and funding. Your sole purpose for organizing a music conference should not be merely for financial gain. For if it is, you may find yourself greatly disappointed. Since, 1998 I have organized the Music Therapy 101 National Music Conference, Workshop and Seminar Series. Some of the workshops have been free while others had a registration price. All the Music Therapy 101 Conferences, Workshops and Seminars were designed to provide a professional atmosphere for networking, negotiating and knowing the business for newcomers and seasoned veterans alike.

Contact us at 800-963-0949 or questions@mt101.com when you have a budget and are ready to start planning your music conference and/or when you are ready to book me for a speaking engagement. We customize packages to suit the needs of our clients. Some of your basic concerns will include the following:

> - Goal of the conference
> - Theme of the conference
> - Conference Name
> - Panel & Workshop Topics
> - Panelists & Speakers to present at the conference
> - Location-City, State, Country
> - Venues-Hotel/Motel, Convention Center, etc.
> - Venues for showcasing talent
> - Date
> - Time of event
> - Attendance Goal
> - Target Market (Conference Demographics)
> - Registration Price
> - Break Even Analysis
> - Sponsorship & Vendor Opportunities
> - Marketing & Promotions Plan & Budget
> - Website Design & Layout

Music Conference Listing

Every music conference below provides a unique opportunity for you to network, negotiate and know the business of music. I intentionally did not include the dates, locations or genre that music each conference caters to, as they tend to change from time to time. Remember to tell the conference organizer you found them in the Music Industry Connection- The Truth about Record Pools & Music Conferences, Talent Shows & Open Mic Book by JaWar.

- A&R Music1.com, LLC.
  2132 Sara Ashley Way, Suite 300 Lithonia, GA 30058
  P) 770-686-9100
  www.arlive.com

- Advanced Music Seminar c/o Oz Music Group, Ltd.
  16 Penn Plaza, Suite 1503, New York, NY 10001
  P) 212-244-2022 P) 800-390-3008 F) 212-244-2166
  www.ams-ny.com
  omg@ozmusicgroup.com

- Americana Music Association
  P.O. Box 128077, Nashville, TN 37212
  411 E. Iris Drive, Suite D, Nashville, TN 37204
  P) 615-386-6936 F) 615-386-6937
  www.americanamusic.org
  info@americanamusic.org

- American Music Conference
  5790 Armada Drive, Carlsbad, CA 92008
  P) 760-431-9124 F) 760-438-7327
  www.amc-music.org
  info@amc-music.org

- Atlantis Music Conference
  1339 Canton Rd., Suite E, Marietta, GA 30066
  P) 770-499-8600 F) 770-499-8650

www.atlantismusic.com

- BESLA-Black Entertainment & Sports Law Association
  P.O. Box 441485, Fort Washington, MD 20749
  P) 301-248-1818 F) 301-248-0700
  www.besla.org
  beslamailbox@aol.com

- Billboard Special Events
  770 Broadway 6th Fl., New York, NY 10003
  P) 646-654-4660 F) 646-654-4674
  www.billboard.com
  bbevents@billboard.com

- CIA-Christian Indie Artists Summit
  P.O. Box 1628, Franklin, TN 37065
  P) 615-594-0426 F) 615-523-1400
  www.ciasummit.com
  info@ciasummit.com

- Chicago Mob Fest
  1658 N. Milwaukee Ave. Ste 292, Chicago, IL 60647
  www.chicagomobfest.com
  info@chicagomobfest.com

- Christian Music Summit
  4227 S. Meridian Suite C275, Puyallup, WA 98373
  P) 253-770-0650 F) 253) 435-5775
  www.ChristianMusicSummit.com
  info@christianmusiciansummit.com

- CMJ Network-College Music Journal
  151 W. 25th St. 12th Fl., New York, NY 10001
  P) 917-606-1908 F) 917-606-1914
  www.cmj.com
  marathon@cmj.com

- CBMR-Conference on Black Music Research
  600 South Michigan Ave., Chicago, IL 60605

P) 312-344-7559 F) 312-344-8029
www.cbmr.org

- College Music Society
312 East Pine Street, Missoula, MT 59802
P) 406-721-9616 F) 406-721-9419
cms@music.org

- Connexion Festival
136 7th Ave South, Jacksonville Beach, FL 32250
P) 904-242-4630
www.connexionfestival.com
lrovero@connexionfestival.com

- COPE – Club Owners, Promoters, Entertainment
Executives & Entrepreneurs
1800 Buckeye St., Atlanta, GA 30310
www.clubcope.org

- Country Radio Seminar (Broadcasters)
819 18th Ave. South Nashville, TN 37203
P) 615-327-4487
www.crb.org

- Cutting Edge/Music Business Institute
1524 North Claiborne Avenue
New Orleans, LA 70116
P) 504-945-1800 F) 504-945-1873
www.jass.com/cuttingedge/
cut_edge@bellsouth.net

- Dewey Beach Fest
113 Dickinson Street, Dewey Beach, DE 19971
P) 717-234-4342 P) 302-227-1209
www.deweybeachfest.com
vwalls@deweybeachfest.com

- Diversafest
P.O. Box 33141, Tulsa, Oklahoma 74153

P) 918-640-9519
www.dfest.com
tgreen@dfest.com

- DIY-Do It Yourself Convention
  3662 Lowry Rd., Los Angeles, CA 90027
  P) 323-665-8080 F) 323-665-8068
  www.diyconvention.com
  diyreporter@diyreporter.com

- Folk Alliance
  510 S. Main St., Memphis, TN 38103
  P) 901-522-1170
  www.folk.org

- Future of Music Policy Summit Coalition
  1615 L Street, NW, Suite 520, Washington, D.C. 20036
  P) 202-429-8855 F) 202-429-8857
  www.futureofmusic.org

- Future Stars Music Conference
  1646 Collingwood Drive, SE, Marietta, GA 30067
  P) 770-217-3762
  www.futurestarsmusicconference.com
  info@futurestarsmusicconference.com

- Gospel Music Association
  1205 Division Street, Nashville, TN 37203
  P) 615-242-0303 F) 615-254-9755
  www.gospelmusic.org

- GMWA – Gospel Music Workshop of America
  3908 West Warren, Detroit, MI 48208
  P) 313-898-6900
  www.gmwanational.org
  manager@gmwanational.org

- Hip Hop Music Business Youth Conference
  925 B Peachtree St. #320, Atlanta, GA 30309

P) 404-484-5538 F) 404-659-9976
www.hiphopyouthconference.com
formeprogram@aol.com

- How Can I Be Down
  2270 DeFoor Hills Road, NE, Atlanta, GA 30318
  P) 404-352-3338 F) 404-352-3394
  www.howcanibedown.com

- IAJE - International Association for Jazz Education
  P.O. Box 724, Manhattan, KS 66505
  P) 785-776-8744 F) 785-776-6190
  www.iaje.org
  info@iaje.org

- Independence Music Conference
  304 Main Ave., PMB 287, Norwalk, CT 06851
  P) 203-606-4649
  www.gopmc.com

- International DJ Expo
  25 Willowdale Ave., Port Washington, NY 11050
  P) 516-767-2500 F) 516-767-9335
  www.djtimes.com

- IEBA-International Entertainment Buyers Association
  PO Box 128376, Nashville, TN 37212
  P) 615-463-0161 F) 615-463-0163
  www.ieba.org
  info@ieba.org

- LAMC-Latin American Music Conference
  c/o Mundo Rockero
  P.O. Box 777, South Gate, CA 90280
  F) 323-564-2518
  www.mundorockero.com
  staff@mundorockero.com

- Listen and Exchange

7322 SW Frwy, Suite 1100
P.O. Box 420567, Houston, TX 77242
P) 713-981-3861 F) 713-878-4526
www.listenandexchange.com
DEDRADAVIS@musiclw.com

- Miami Music Media - M3 Summit
  594 Broadway, Suite 1212, New York, NY 10012
  P) 212-226-5304 F) 212-274-9899
  www.m3summit.com
  info@m3summit.com

- Mid-Atlantic Music Conference
  5588 Chamblee Dunwoody Road #110
  Dunwoody, GA 30338
  P) 770-300-0175 P) 888-755-0036
  www.midatlanticmusic.com

- Mid-Point Music Festival
  8413 Burns Ave., Cincinnati, OH 45126
  P) 877-572-8690
  www.mpmf.com
  info@mpmf.com

- MMS-Midwest Music Summit
  PO Box 47038, Indianapolis, IN 46247
  P) 317-536-6151 F) 317-222-1828
  www.midwestmusicsummit.com
  registration@midwestmusicsummit.com

- Millennium Music Conference
  P.O. Box 1012, Harrisburg, PA 17108
  P) 717-221-1124 F) 717-221-1159
  www.musicconference.net
  info@musicconference.net

- Million Dollar Record Pool Conference

2459 Roosevelt Hwy. Suite B-1, College Park GA 30337
P) 404-766-1275 F) 404-559-0117
http://mildol.com
mde@mildol.com

- Mississippi Hip Hop Conference
  P.O. Box 8465, Columbus, MS 39705
  P) 662-251-0075 F) 888-474-6137
  info@newpowermagazine.com

- Motor City Music Conference
  512 S.Washington Ave., #237, Royal Oak, MI 48067
  P) 248-797-2348
  www.motorcitymusic.com
  info@motorcitymusic.com

- Music Player Network
  2800 Campus Drive, San Mateo, CA 94403
  P) 650-513-4340 F) 650-513-4646
  www.musicplayer.com
  vpippin@musicplayer.com

- **MT101-Music Therapy 101**
  P.O. Box 52682, Atlanta, GA 30355
  P) 800-963-0949
  www.mt101.com
  questions@mt101.com

- Music Teachers National Association
  441 Vine St., Ste. 505, Cincinnati, Ohio, 45202
  P) 513-421-1420
  www.mtna.org

- NAMM-International Music Products Association
  5790 Armada Drive, Carlsbad, CA 92008
  P) 760-438-8001 P) 800-767-6266 F) 760-438-7327
  www.namm.com
  info@namm.com

- NARIP-National Association of Record Industry Professionals
  P.O. Box 2446, Toluca Lake, CA 91610
  P) 818-769-7007
  www.narip.com
  info@narip.com

- Nashville Songwriter's Festival
  511 Beech Creek Rd., Waverly, TN 37185
  P) 931-296-4067 P) 615-424-1491
  www.songwritersfestival.com
  info@songwritersfestival.com

- National Association for Music Education
  1806 Robert Fulton Drive, Reston, VA 20191
  P) 800-336-3768 F) 703-860-1531
  www.menc.org

- Nemo Music Conference
  312 Stuart St., 4th Floor, Boston, MA 02116
  P) 617-348-2899 F) 617-348-2383
  www.nemoboston.com
  info@nemoboston.com

- NMC-New Media Consortium
  2499 S Capital of Texas Hwy
  Building A, Suite 202, Austin, TX 78746
  P) 512-445-4200 F) 512-445-4205
  www.nmc.org
  info@nmc.org

- Radio & Records
  2049 Century Park East, 41st Floor
  Los Angeles, CA 90067
  P) 310-553-4330 F) 310-203-9763
  www.radioandrecords.com

- Rockgirl Music Conference
  7683 SE 27th St., #317, Mercer Island, WA 98040

F) 206-624-7097
www.rockgrl.com
orders@rockgrl.com

- Soul Music Summit
  2870 Peachtree Rd., Suite 404, Atlanta, GA 30305
  P) 678-613-6260
  www.soulsummitonline.com
  terry.bello@gmail.com

- SUMC-Southeast Urban Music Conference
  P.O. Box 670296, Marietta, GA 30066
  P) 770-621-5820 F) 770-973-0136
  www.smiurban.com
  smiurban@comcast.net

- SXSW-South by Southwest
  P.O. Box 4999, Austin, TX 78765
  P) 512-467-7979 F) 512-451-0754
  www.sxsw.com
  sxsw@sxsw.com

- Tampa Music Conference
  7530-G Waters Ave., Tampa, FL 33615
  P) 813-880-8384
  www.tmconf.com

- TapeOpCon
  270 S. Stoner Ave., Tucson, AZ 85748
  www.tapeopcon.com

- Texas Summer Music Conference
  1700 Commerce St. Suite 1900, Dallas, TX 75201
  P) 214-749-0134 F) 214-749-0130
  www.texassummermusicconference.com
  themoves@sbcglobal.net

- The Power Summit
  665 Broadway, Suite 801, New York, NY 10012

P) 212-375-6211 F) 212-375-6205
www.mixshowpowersummit.com

- The Rated Next Convention c/o *One Two Productions*
  3699 Wilshire Blvd., Suite 850, Los Angeles, CA 90010
  P) 818-679-9759
  www.ratednext1.com
  ratednext1@yahoo.com

- Thirsty Melon
  P.O. Box 339, Taylorsville, KY 40071-0339
  P) 877-307-6418
  www.thirstymelon.com
  info@thirstymelon.com

- TJsDJs Quarterly Record Pool Conference
  1424 Capital Circle NW, Tallahassee, FL 32303
  P) 850-878-3634 F) 850-877-3110
  www.tjsdjs.com

- Uplifting Minds
  c/o Freelance Associates
  P.O. Box 36876, Los Angeles, CA 90036
  www.upliftingminds2.com

- Urban Network
  3255 Wilshire Blvd., Suite 815, Los Angeles, CA 90010
  P) 213-388-4155 F) 213-388-0034
  www.urbannetwork.com

- VMC-Virgnia Music Conference
  1559 S.13th South, Arlington, VA 22204
  www.vamusicconference.com

- West Coast Song Writers
  1724 Laurel St., Suite #120, San Carlos, CA 94070
  P) 650-654-3966 P) 800-FOR-SONG F) 650-654-2156
  info@westcoastsongwriters.org
  www.westcoastsongwriters.org

- Winter Music Conference
  3450 NE 12th Terrace, Fort Lauderdale, FL 33334
  P) 954-563-4444 F) 954-563-1599
  www.wintermusicconference.com
  info@wintermusicconference.com

- World Forum on Music
  c/o Department of Cultural Affairs, City of Los Angeles
  201 North Figueroa Street, Suite 1400
  Los Angeles, CA 90012
  P) 213-202-5500
  www.worldforumonmusic.com
  info@worldforumonmusic.com

- Baltimore Music Conference
  www.baltimoremusicconference.com

- Bay Area Music Conference
  www.gtpfam.com

- Carolina CD & Record Pool Quarterly Explosion
  www.entertainment4life.com

- Core DJs Retreat
  www.coredjs.com

- Digital Summit
  www.digitalsummit.org

- Durango Songwriters Expo
  www.durangosong.com

- Dynamic Producer
  www.dynamicproducer.com

- Far West Regional Folk Alliance
  www.far-west.org

- Florida Entertainment Summit

www.floridaentertainmentsummit.com

- Florida Music Festival
  www.flordiamusicfestival.com

- Global Entertainment and Media Summit
  www.globalentertainmentnetwork.com

- Hood Magazine Music Conference
  www.hoodnetworkmeeting.com

- I Create Music: ASCAP Expo
  www.ascap.com/expo

- I Rock the Mic
  www.irockthemic.com

- Jack Da Juice
  www.jackdajuice.com

- Jax Music Conference & A&R Super Summit
  www.jaxmusicconference.com

- Kauai Music Festival
  www.kauaimusicfestival.com

- Music Expo
  www.musicexpo.net

- Music Law Conference
  www.musiclawconference.com

- Music Talk Sessions
  www.musictalksessions.com

- OG Ron Houston Music Conference
  www.ogronchoustonmusicconference.com

- PAUMS-PA Urban Music Summit
  www.paums.com

- Southern Entertainment Awards & Conference
  www.southernentawards.com

- Southern Regional Ent. & Sports Law/IP Conference
  www.selaw.org

- South Park Music Festival & Conference
  www.southparkmusic.com

- Summer Music Conference
  www.summermusicconference.net

- The Composer Expo
  www.tcmcomposerexpo.com

- The Copyright Society of the U.S.A (Annual Meeting)
  www.csusa.org

- The Industry Connection Music Conference
  www.eleganceentertainment.com

- The Powers of Music Seminar & Showcase
  www.thepowersofmusic.com

- Vegas Music Conference
  www.eamc.us

RECORD POOLS

What is a record pool?

A record pool is a DJ Membership organization that gives you cost-effective access to mix show, club and mobile DJs. A mix show DJ spins on radio. Mix show DJs tend to play new music before the music gets added to the stations regular rotation. A club DJ spins at a particular club servicing the clubs patrons. Mobile DJs tend to service special occasions such as wedding receptions, private parties and so forth. DJs pay dues monthly, quarterly or yearly to be a record pool member. Once members pay their dues, they receive new music in CD, Vinyl or MP3 formats. Normally, the DJs are required to give feedback or listener response to the pool director in a timely fashion. For instance, the DJs may report to the pool director once a week. Once the DJs have sent in their feedback reports, the pool director compiles a chart list that is distributed to record companies via fax and/or email. The chart list is sent regularly. For example, it may be sent once a week or twice a month. Record pools are one of the most cost-effective ways to generate a buzz, monitor a potential hit and test before you press. Toward the end of this book is a list of over 130 United States Record Pools.

Is a record pool right for my music?

Most DJs in record pools tend to play music that is played for audiences that dance or club music. If you create or promote dance, house, hip-hop, R&B music etc. your music is probably suited for record pools. However, if you create and promote music such as country, but can't locate a country record pool, this might be an opportunity for you to make your mark in the industry, while creating an additional stream of revenue by starting a country record pool.

What does it mean to service a record pool?

Servicing a record pool simply means to send the pool your music in whatever format it request. Some pools require vinyl, CDs or MP3's.

Does it cost money to service a record pool?

Most record pools don't charge a fee to service (send music to) their DJs. If you have an undeniable hit and are actively promoting your music, then most of the DJs will play it, as they want to have bragging rights as the DJ that "broke" (played first) your record in their market. While most pools don't charge to service their DJs, some do charge a stocking fee. Normally, the fee is nominal and the argument is that it keeps some of the fly by night labels from sending a lot of music that the label has no real intention on promoting.

Many record pools have quarterly DJ meetings and offer label's opportunities to sponsor the events. Record pools also offer additional marketing and promotions campaigns. While sponsoring a pool's DJ meeting is not necessary, it will keep you on the mind of DJ members and the record pool director. Sponsorship could be achieved at various levels including money, t-shirts, DJ bags, hats and lunch for the DJs, etc.

Always keep your receipts as these expenses are of a business nature and tend to be tax deductible. However, you will want to consult with your tax professional or C.P.A. (Certified Public Accountant), as I am not a tax professional and do not provide tax advice. You may find a tax professional or accountant by asking for referrals from others in the business, looking in your local phone book or the Internet.

How to know if a record pool is legit?

Contact the record pool director and ask them which record companies regularly service them with priority artist and/or new music. Contact major label promotions departments and ask them which record pools they regularly service with new music. Ask other independent labels in your area which record pools they would recommend . Also, you may ask to get on the record pools fax or email list, so you can start receiving updated chart position from the pools. Overtime you will determine which pools are legit by how consistent their lists are. Many pools now post their chart position on their website.

Record pools should have no problem letting you know which labels regularly service them with new music. Many record pools have become full service marketing and promotions companies for independent and major labels. Often, they will attempt to sell you on these additional marketing services. Because of a pools access to a number of working club, mix show and mobile DJs and its street credibility, it may be worth considering hiring a record pool to give your release that added push it needs to become a break out record.

I'm a DJ, should I join a record pool?

Joining a record pool may be a great way for a DJ to get new music before everyone else does (given that established record companies actively service the record pool.) In addition, joining the right record pool could increase the DJs network and notoriety by their peers and the industry at large. At the end of the day this is all done to bring the DJ more paying gigs, additional revenue streams and to create additional windows of opportunity for long-term success. For instance, some DJs move from DJing at a club or mix show to becoming a record producer or DJing while on the road for an established recording artist.

Traditionally, DJs joined record pools to get music for free for which they would otherwise have to pay. Initially, the major labels did not fully appreciate the club and mobile DJs ability to break a new artist. Through a record pool the DJs were able to form an alliance or coalition and were able to demonstrate their ability to promote new releases or test before the label pressed mass quantities of new music. Remember the old adage that there is strength in numbers.

Some DJs have gotten extremely business savvy, validated there worth and built a proven track record by using Mix CDs and the Internet to gain cult like followings. As such, some DJs have moved away from becoming paying members of record pools to forming DJ companies where major and independent labels now pay them to promote their artist and singles. These DJs have been successful at building their brand, marketing and promoting themselves and their respective clients. Funkmaster Flex and DJ Drama are two DJs that have been extremely successful at building their brand and have gone to do more than merely DJing a club night. However, before a DJ reaches this point it may be wise to join a record pool to get free records and for the networking opportunities.

What should I ask before joining a record pool?

You should ask the price of joining and maintaining membership in a particular record pool. You may want to ask how you will receive new music, how often will you get it and what is required of you. In addition, ask if there any other perks or advantages to becoming a member of one record pool over another. This is important to consider because the list in this book has over 130 record pools in the United States and while all pools provide a similar service not all pools are alike. You will want to speak with other DJs and ask them to tell you why they chose one pool over the next. This should give you additional direction and questions to ask before joining any pool.

What is the cost for being a member?

The price varies from pool to pool. However, DJs may expect to pay anywhere from $100-$300 a month to be a member of a record pool. Keep in mind that the price of being a DJ record pool member should be directly related to the established number of labels that consistently service the pool with new music.

DJs record pool dues are a business expense and should be treated as such. DJs should consult their tax professional or C.P.A. (Certified Public Accountant) to learn the best way to treat this business expense.

How many records will I get per month?

That truly depends on the record pool. Obviously, the more established and larger pools will receive and distribute more music to its DJs than a relatively new and unknown pool will.

How will I receive my records/CDs?

Most record pools have regular meetings where they distribute new music to their DJ members. Some pools have started emailing MP3's to their DJs and allowing the DJs to burn their own copies, thereby reducing shipping cost and time. Of course, this only works for DJs who spin CDs. If a DJ merely spins vinyl, then emailing an MP3 will not work. Record pools may also ship its' members new music via a freight service such as UPS or FedEx.

41

What am I required to do?

As a DJ member you may be asked to play new music once or twice in your respective venue. If you are a club DJ you will be asked to give the record a spin during your club night. However, if you are a mobile DJ you may be asked to spin the record at the most appropriate time. In addition, you will need to record listener response and send feedback results to the record pool director. Some pools have meetings that require the DJs attendance, however, these meetings tend to be held only quarterly and normally serve as great networking tools that may help advance the career of a DJ.

What is the difference between a mix show, club and mobile DJ?

A mix show DJ spins on radio. Mix show DJs tend to play new music before the music gets added to the stations regular rotation. A club DJ spins at a particular club servicing the clubs patrons. Mobile DJs tend to service special occasions such as wedding receptions, private parties and so forth.

HOW TO USE RECORD POOLS TO TEST-MARKET YOUR NEXT HIT

Record pools are DJ membership organizations that give you cost-effective access to radio, club and mobile DJs. Essentially, DJs pay either a monthly, quarterly or yearly dues to be a record pool member. In exchange for paying membership dues the record pool distributes new music to the DJs in either CD or vinyl formats. Normally, the DJs are required to give feedback or listener response to the pool director in a timely fashion. For instance, the DJs may report to the pool director once a week. When the DJs have sent in their feedback reports, the pool director compiles a chart list that is distributed to record companies via fax and/or email. The chart list is sent regularly. For instance, it may be sent once a week or twice a month. Record pools are one of the most cost-effective ways to either generate a buzz or monitor a potential hit. It should be noted that record pools tend to work best for styles of music that are played in clubs i.e. Dance, Hip Hop, R&B, Pop and Trip Hop, etc. One of the reasons that there may be a Club or Dance Remix to a song is so it may be played in a nightclub setting.

Many record pools have regular meetings either bi-weekly, monthly or quarterly. *Actively attending* these meetings is a fantastic way to meet the DJs that can help break your record. By "actively attending", I mean attending these meetings prepared to network. For instance, make sure that you have business cards, flyers and other promotional material to distribute to everyone at the meeting. I attended the Leaders of Development Record Pool Meeting in Atlanta and was able to give a few copies of my newspaper the **MIC (Music Industry Connection)** to Greg Street. Greg is one of the top radio-personalities in Atlanta, Georgia and Dallas, Texas yet he was very approachable during the meeting. Because record pool meetings are music business events most people are receptive to networking. It has been my experience that record pool meetings are some of the best places to meet industry tastemakers in your own backyard.

In addition to networking with industry tastemakers in your own backyard, record pool meetings are an excellent way to get immediate response from DJs about your new music. DJs tend to be very honest when giving feedback about new music at these events. Some of the record pool meetings offer live talent showcases for artists to perform.. While sponsorship (paying money) is normally required to perform in the record pool talent showcases, it usually is worth the investment to perform in front of the DJs that can help propel your career. **Remember to treat everyone that you meet like they are the most important person on earth.** Not only will this move your career forward faster, but more importantly, it will help you have more fun in a cutthroat industry. In addition, you never know whom you may be talking to; it could be a radio station music/program director or editor of a music magazine. This is especially true when you begin attending record pool meetings outside your home market.

Now, let's say that you are an independent record company in Atlanta, Georgia and you're preparing to release a CD. Before spending all your advertising dollars in Atlanta, you will want to test-market your first single using record pools in Georgia, Alabama, South Carolina and Florida. After a few weeks you might find that your single is getting a so-so response in Atlanta, but in Birmingham, Alabama and South Carolina your single has the potential of being this year's summer hit! Since, Birmingham and South Carolina are only a two and three hour drive from Atlanta, respectively, it might make good sense to spend more of your advertising dollars in those areas. In the *Atlanta Music Industry Connection and Los Angeles Music Industry Connection Books* I go into detail on "How to Promote Your Independent Release". This will increase your opportunities for creating a street buzz faster and turning a profit sooner via CD, concert ticket and merchandising sales.

Before spending you hard earned money from your day job pursuing your music career at night, consider record pools as a cost-effective method of test-marketing your next hit.

You may get a copy of either the *Atlanta Music Industry Connection or Los Angeles Music Industry Connection Book* by completing the order form in the back of the book or visiting www.mt101.com. Below is a list of record pools in the United States.

Record Pool Listing

ALABAMA

- RW Record pool
  799 Baltimore Hill Rd., Huntsville, AL 35810
  P) 256-859-1851 P) 205-305-3680
  Rwrecordpool2@aol.com

- Southern Network Association
  207 Montgomery ST # 300, Montgomery, AL 36104
  P) 334-834-9262 F) 334-262-4924
  Snaent@aol.com

ARIZONA

- Desert West Music Promotion
  3936 W Grant, Phoenix, AZ 85009
  P) 602-484-0242 F) 602-595-7516
  Dwpromotion@cox.net

CALIFORNIA

- American Record Pool
  3540 Wilshire Blvd., Suite 834, Los Angeles, CA 90010
  F) 310-659-7856
  amrecpool@aol.com

- B.A.S.S. Record Pool

36488 Fremont Blvd., Fremont, CA 94536
P) 510-739-1862 F) 510-739-1893
bassrecordpool@aol.com

- BADDA
  Pier 31, San Francisco, CA 94111
  P) 415-882-9700 F) 415-882-9862
  baddadjs@aol.com

- California Music Business Entertainment
  6532 Garber Ave., San Diego, CA 92139
  P) 619-470-3111 F) 619-470-3231
  Bmg925@hotmail.com

- Cue's Record Pool
  6340 Mission St., Daly City, CA 94014
  P) 650-755-1110 F) 650-755-1115
  djcue@aol.com

- En La Casa DJ's Record Pool
  590 Metaxa Ct., Santa Rosa, CA 95407
  P) 707-545-9359 F) 707-545-9387
  tazzytaz@enlacasa.com

- Four Star Record Pool
  610 16th St., Suite #221, Oakland, CA 94612
  P) 510-839-4435 F) 510-839-5301
  tbutler@4starrecordpool.com

- Getobaby Record Pool
  2510 ½ W. Sunset Blvd., Los Angeles, CA 90026
  P) 213-483-2451 F) 213-483-2435
  calikingz@aol.com

- Global Record Pool
  1588 Arrow Unit F, La Verne, CA 91750
  P) 909-593-9244 F) 909-593-9242
  www.globalrecordpool.com
  luckylou@globalrecordpool.com

- Green House Record Pool
  1680 N. Vine St., #1119, Los Angeles, CA 90028
  P) 323-466-5141 F) 323-466-5121

- Heavyweights Record Pool
  14706 Aranza Dr., La Mirada, CA 90638
  P) 888-998-2041

- Impact Record Pool
  4055 McClung Dr., Los Angeles, CA 90008
  P) 323-292-2022 F) 323-298-0913
  www.impactrecordpool.com
  fut@impactrecordpool.com

- Inland Empire Record Pool
  114 Oaktree Dr., Perris, CA 92571
  P) 909-657-3277 F) 909-657-8225
  billspool@aol.com

- International Record Source
  665 H St., Suite C, Chula Vista, CA 91910
  P) 619-476-1288 F) 619-476-1295

- Jamz City Record Pool
  2410 N. Michael St., Visalia, CA 93291
  P) 209-733-3132 F) 209-733-3230

- LADJ Association
  5261 Hollywood Blvd., Los Angeles, CA 90027
  P) 213-463-5235 F) 213-463-4211
  ladj@earthlink.net

- Mixx-N-Company Record Pool
  1731 Howe Ave., Suite 474, Sacramento, CA 95825
  P) 800-971-MIXX P) 916-ITS-MIXX F) 916-489-FAX
  mixxncompany@aol.com

- Pacific Coast DJ Association

3315 E. Second St., Long Beach, CA 90803
P) 562-434-7603

- Resource Record Pool
  8350 Melrose Ave., Ste 10, Los Angeles, CA 90069
  P) 323-651-2085 F) 323-655-5223
  resourcepromo@aol.com

- RITMO International Record Pool
  790 Shotweil St., San Francisco, CA 94110
  P) 415-821-3563 F) 415-821-1521
  Ritmo100@aol.com

- San Diego Disc Jockey Association
  365 W. Second Ave., #216, Econdido, CA 92025
  P) 619-489-5266 F) 619-489-6959

- SOBAD Record Pool
  65 Post St., San Jose, CA 95113
  P) 408-277-0111 F) 408-277-0123
  sobad@sobad-djs.com

- Soul Disco Record Pool
  1643 Bush Piedmont, Suite 318, Oakland, CA 94611
  P) 510-729-8087 F) 510-428-9132

- Soundworks Record Pool
  228 Valencia St., San Francisco, CA 94103
  P) 415-487-3980 F) 415-487-1972
  sndwrks@best.com

- The Pros Record Pool
  440 Grand Ave., Oakland, CA 94610
  P) 510-839-3000 F) 510-839-3201
  www.thepros.com
  info@thepros.com

- Ultra Soundz Record Pool
  482 San Mateo Ave., Sun Bruno, CA 94066

P) 650-871-7348 F) 650-871-4218
ultradjs@aol.com

- Wordlife Record Pool
  4845 Fountain Suite #1080, Los Angeles, CA 90029
  P) 323-402-1231
- Xtreme Record Pool
  2425 Channing Way, Suite #223, Berkley, CA 94704
  icewater@onebox.com

COLORADO

- Dancing Discs of Discs of Denver
  2408 E. Colfax Ave., Denver, CO 80206
  P) 303-333-6901 F) 303-333-0237
  butter3d@aol.aom

CONNECTICUT

- Connecticut's Music Pool
  1440 Whaley Ave., Suite # 172, New Haven, CT 06515
  P) 203-789-0038 F) 203-789-1166
  ctmuzic@aol.com

- Beats Per Minute Record Pool
  20 Butternut Knoil Middletown, CT 06457
  P) 860-344-9449 F) 860-632-5530
  Bpmconnect1@aol.com

- BPM CT SELECT
  337 Newington Rd., W Hartford, CT 06110
  P) 860-250-1514 F) 860-232-3402
  markiemint@yahoo.com

DELAWARE

- First State Record Pool
  3207 B Miller Rd. Wilmington, DE 19803
  P) 302-292-0983 F) 302-292-0983

Firststatercordpool@yahoo.com

FLORIDA

- 904 Record Pool
  1828 Nektonic, Tallahassee, FL, 32304
  P) 850-575-8519 F) 850-574-8427
  Pool904@gnv.fdt.net

- Amlando Record Pool
  4270 Aloma Ave. #124 Suite #45-A
  Winter Park, FL 32792
  P) 407-671-5272 F) 509-472-4972
  djinfinite@msn.com

- Flamingo Music Promotions
  1450 N.E. 123 St. Suite#113 Miami, FL 33161
  P) 303-895-1246 F) 305-895-0913
  FlamingoRecpool@aol.com

- Florida Sun Coast Record Pool
  7747 63rd St. N. Pinellas Park, FL 33781
  P) 727-544-7609 F) 727-545-5371
  Flasuncoastrp@aol.com

- Fort Lauderdale/Miami Record Pool
  3450 N.E. 12th Terrace Ft. Lauderdale, FL 33334
  P) 954-563-3888 F) 954-563-6889
  FortlaudRP@aol.com

- Full Fledge Record Pool
  8594 Tansy Dr., Orlando, FL 32819
  P) 917-531-9836

- Hitz Music Promotions
  1205 Washington Avenue, Miami Beach FL 35139
  P) 305-604-5915 F) 305-532-4498
  ad1972@aol.com

- Majestic Sands Dance Pool
  8410 W. Flagler St #210 B, Miami, FL 33144
  P) 305-567-2900 F) 305-559-4818

- Miami Urban Record CD Pool
  444 Brickeil Ave, Miami, FL 33131
  P) 305-358-4563 F) 305-358-3836

- Rhythm City Record Pool
  14991 N.E 18th Ave N, Miami, Fl 33181
  P) 305-931-5695 F) 305-940-0076
  DJJUICE72@aol.com

- TJ's DJ's Record Pool
  1424 NW Capital Circle, Tallahassee, FL 32302
  P) 850-877-6090 F) 850-670-3110
  www.tjsdjs.com
  tjsdjs@tjsdjs.com

- Top Wonder Pool
  1431 N. W. 31st Ave Ste. 10, Ft. Lauderdale, FL 33311
  P) 954-485-5980 F) 954-485-0497

- Upstart Entertainment & Record Pool
  4446 Hendricks Avenue Suite, Jacksonville, FL 32207
  P) 904-448-9211 F) 904-739-9494
  www.upstart-entertainment.com
  upstartrecordpool@comcast.net

GEORGIA

- Aphilliates, LLC
  P.O. Box 4596, Atlanta, GA 30302
  P) 404-524-1266 F) 404-524-1267
  www.theaphilliates.com

- Atlanta Urban Mix
  131 Walker Street, Suite-B, Atlanta, GA 30313
  P) 404-589-1126 F) 404-589-1127 Cell) 404-966-1847

www.atlantaurbanmix.com
msmoak@atlantaurbanmix.com

- Big City DJ's CD-Pool
  4660 Cedar Keys Lane, Stone Mountain, GA 30083
  P) 404-501-0220 Cell) 404-867-9133
  www.bigcitydjs.com
  pooldirector@bigcitydjs.com

- Certified Star DJs
  Attn: Tonya "Lady T" Wheeler
  3044 Briarcliff Rd., Suite, 8, Atlanta, GA 30338
  P) 404-514-4758 P) 678-732-4915
  www.certifiedstardjs.com
  allstarzent@yahoo.com

- Digital DJs, LLC
  8725 Roswell Rd, Suite O-166, Atlanta, GA 30350
  P) 732-979-3338
  www.digital-djs.com
  info@digital-djs.com

- Dixie Dance Kings Record Pool
  42 Milton Ave., Alpharetta, GA 30004
  P) 770-740-0356 P) 770-740-0357 P) 770-667-0305
  P) 888-649-5625 F) 770-740-0358
  www.dancekings.com
  ddkings@aol.com

- Hittmen DJs
  2214 April Lane, Decatur, GA 30035
  P) 404-328-8823
  www.hittmendjslive.com

- Jumpin Jack Record Pool
  970 Park Gate Place, Stone Mountain, GA 30083
  P) 770-413-9339 P) 404-663-1130
  recordpool@go.com
  wali_56@yahoo.com

- L.O.D. (Legion of Doom) Record Pool
  5319 Old National Hwy., College Park, GA 30349
  P) 404-684-5898 P) 404-392-9415 F) 404-684-5973
  www.lodrecordpool.com
  info@lodrecordpool.com

- Million Dollar Record Pool
  2459 Roosevelt Hwy., Ste B-1 College Park, GA 30337
  P) 404-766-1275 F) 404-559-0117
  www.mildol.com
  mde@mildol.com

- The Higher Ground – Atlanta Chapter
  P.O. Box 1126, Lithonia, GA 30058
  P) 888-571-3999
  www.highergroundrecordpool.org
  djlace@highergroundrecordpool.org

HAWAII

- Hawaii DJ Association
  2570 S. Beretania St. Suite #103 Honolulu, HI 96826
  P) 808-946-3770 F) 808-964-3771
  thebeat@hawaii.rr.com

ILLINOIS

- Illinois Record Pool
  3625 W. 125th St. Chicago, IL 60803
  P) 708-389-9629 F) 708-389-9628
  Ilrecpool@aol.com

- Larlin Music Association
  16736 S. Merrill Ave: South Holland, IL 60473
  P) 708-895-8900

- Lets Dance Music Pool
  3711 N. Ashland Ave. 2nd Flr, Chicago, IL 60613
  P) 773-525-7553 F) 773-525-098

- St. Louis Metro DJ Association
  313 N Buchanan, Edwardsville, Il 62025
  P) 618-656-4831
  simdja@ezl.com

- Urban Force DJ Pool
  500 W Cermak Rd, Ste 512, Chicago, Il 60616
  P) 312-226-8722 F) 312-226-0032
  urbanforce@aol.com

- V.I.P Chicago
  3505 W Fullerton, Chicago, Il 60647
  P) 773-772-5570 F) 773-772-6059
  www.vipchicago.com
  info@vipchicago.com

KENTUCKY

- Five Star Record Pool
  504 Garrard St. Covington, KY 41011
  P) 859-261-6972
  fivestarrp@aol.com

- Soul City Sounds Record Pool
  2933 East Hill Dr., Lexington, KY 40515
  P) 859-608-8550 F) 859-253-8823
  Soulcity@gte.net

MARYLAND

- Direct Drive Record Pool
  1801 Fails Rd. suite # 3C Baltimore, MD 21201
  P) 410-225-3376 F) 410-244-0293
  DDRP1200@aol.com

- Mid-Atlantic Dance-Promotions/GBRP
  2112 Maryland Ave, Lower Baltimore, MD 21218
  P) 410-727-7949 F) 775-305-7677
  gary@madpromotions.com

- Tables Of Distinction
  630 Sheridan St Ste 218, Hyattsville, MD 20783
  P) 301-270-2604 F) 301-270-5752
  eardrum@juno.com

MASSACHUSETTS

- Boston Record Pool
  214 Harvard Ave. Alston, MA 02134
  P) 617-731-1500 F) 617-227-433
  MarkBRPool@aol.com

- Groove Pool Boston DJ Association
  84 High St. suite#7 Medford, MA 02155
  P) 781-393-4449 F) 781-395-2027
  Jtoto@groovepool.com

- Mass Pool DJ Association
  30A Revere Beach Parkway revere, MA 02151
  P) 617-796-6596 F) 617-569-2900
  Masspool@masspool.com

- New England DJ Association
  72-74 E. Dedham St., Suite # 5, Boston, MA 02118
  P) 617-695-9941 F) 617-422-0420
  Nedja@aol.com

MICHIGAN

- Advanced Music Promotions
  815 Mc Lean Avenue Royal Oak, MI 48067
  djmuzik@home.com

- Innovative Jocks Record Pool
  8760 E. Outer Dr. Detroit, MI 48213
  P) 313-371-9228 F) 313-371-4567
  innovativejocks@aol.com

- Midwestern Dance Association

13911 Pfent Ave, Detroit, MI 48205
P) 313-527-1546 F) 313-527-7455
MDAPool@aol.com

- United Dance Music Association
  4816 Seminole St, Detroit, MI 48214
  P) 313-923-2724 F) 313-923-2623
  UDMA1@aol.com

MINNESOTA

- Urban Lights MINN ST Jocks
  1449 University Minneapolis, MN 55104
  P) 612-647-9650 F) 612-647-9669

- Vinyl Cartel Record Pool
  405 West Lake St., Minneapolis, MN 55408
  P) 612-824-0505 F) 612-824-4537
  BRO JULES@aol.com

NEVADA

- Record Systems Record Pool
  3301 Spring Mountain Rd, Las Vegas, NV 89102
  P) 702-227-4001 F) 702-227-4001
  www.recordsystemslv.com
  rorymack@recordsystemslv.com

NEW JERSEY

- Atlantic City Record Pool
  137 E. Nightingale Way Absecon, NJ 08201
  P) 609-652-5071
  Acrecordpool@aol.com

- Philadelphia Spinners Assoc
  15 Beideman Ave Cherry Hill, NJ 08002
  P) 856-662-7222 F) 856-662-6617
  Psa.nj@juno.com

- Progressive Dance Promotion
  8 Mosswood Terrance, Maplewood, NJ 07040
  P) 973-762-5005 F) 973-762-5520
  www.Progressicedancepromotion.com
  pdpp@aol.com

- Ricketts Record Pool
  52 Graham Terrace, Saddle Brook, NJ 07663
  P) 973-478-5764 F) 973-478-7862
  rickett@idt.net

- New Jersey ASSN Of Dance
  1434 Linbarger Ave, Plainfield, NJ 07602
  P) 908-757-0967 F) 908-757-1159

NEW YORK

- Albany NY Assn of DJs
  116 Consumer Square, Ste 377, Plattsburgh, NY 12901
  P) 514-874-1755 F) 514-874-1869
  csipromo@yahoo.com

- Big Dawg Record Pool
  135 W.29th St. Suite # 203 New York, NY 10001
  P) 212-564-7570 F) 212-564-7570
  biggdawwg2002@yahoo.com

- Blazin Vinyl DJ Pool
  266 Elmwood Ave. PMB 369 Buffalo, NY 14222
  P) 416-412-4431 F) 416-412-7487
  Chrisnice@ica.net

- Buffalo New York DJ Association
  73 Strasbourg Dr., Buffalo, NY 14227
  P) 716-668-1136
  BfloDJs@aol.com

- Club Service International Record Pool
  116 Consumer Square Suite#377 Plattsburgh, NY 12901
  P) 514-874-1755 F) 514-874-1869
  www.emcee2total.net

- Buffalo Urban Pool
  25 High St, Buffalo, NY 14209
  P) 716-884-4783F) 716-886-3735
  Radio1122@aol.com

- For The Record
  928 Broadway Suite# 400 New, New York, NY 10010
  P) 212-598-4177 F) 212-505-8041
  fortlaudrp@aol.com

- Franchise/Big Dawg
  276 5th Ave suite#602, New York NY 10001
  P) 212-545-5828 F) 212-545 -5815
  info@4starrecordpool.com

- H.O.T Urban Music Pool
  116 Consumer Square suite#377 Plattsburgh, NY 12901
  P) 514-874-1755 F) 514) 874-1869
  emcee@total.net

- Idlest Sounds Record
  231 Evergreen Ave. Central Lslip, NY 11722
  P) 631-348-0902 F) 631-234-0807
  illestsoundsrecordpool@yahoo.com

- Infinity Record Pool
  4203 Hyman Blvd. Staten Island, NY 10308
  P) 718-967-4793 F) 718-967-4793

- International music center record pool
  330 W. 38th St. Suite #807 New York, NY 10018
  P) 212-2444132 F) 212-244-4134
  imcrp@banet.net

- Long Island Record
  3601 Hempstead Turnpike Levittown, NY 11756
  P) 516-796-6596 F) 516-623-4660
  lilrecordpool@aol.com

- Mix-Master Record Pool
  28 East Hill Drive, Smithtown, NY 11787
  P) 646-425-8342 F) 413-771-0088
  nydj21@aol.com

- MOJO Record Pool
  672 East 24th St, Bronx, NY 10466
  P) 718-881-7396 F) 718-519-7331

- New York Record Pool
  104 West 14th St, 2nd Fl, New York, NY 10011
  P) 212-924-0388 F) 212-924-0388

- Reel Record Pool
  2620 Ditmars Blvd, Astoria, NY 11105
  P) 718-721-4422 F) 718-721-4423

- SOS Dance Pool
  1154 Castle Hill Ave #2, Bronx, NY 10462
  P) 718-829-4000 F) 718-829-4014

- Sound Table DJ Pool
  801 Arnett Boulevard, Rochester, NY 14619
  P) 716-436-7143 F) 716-436-7143
  Soundtable2001@juno.com

- S.U.R.E. Record Pool
  2128 Westchester Ave, Bronx, NY 10462
  P) 718-904-0500 F) 718-904-1799
  www.surererecordpool.com
  surerecord@aol.com

- VIP New York Record Pool
  34 Industrial St-2nd Fl, Bronx, NY 10461

P) 718-931-1210 F) 718-931-1238
viprecords@aol.com

- Vinyl Cartel Record Pool
  511 Avenue Of The Americas PMB 44
  New York, NY 10011
  P) 212-208-0961 F) 212-208-2487
  info@vinylcartel.com

NORTH CAROLINA

- Hitbound Music International
  P.O. Box 657, Castle Hayne, NC 28429
  P) 910-675-3873 C) 910-538-9364 F) 910-675-8487
  hmirecpool@aol.com

- New Music Promotions
  2106 Wintergreen Place, Durham, NC 27707
  P) 919-596-9805 F) 919-596-5725

- Starfleet Music Pool
  3521 Mallard Cove Ct, Charlotte, NC 28269
  P) 704-599-6645 F) 704-599-1863
  captkirk@starfleetmusic.com

- Triangle Record Pool
  4529 Draper Rd, Raleigh, NC 27604
  P) 919-834-6811 F) 919-878-3400

OHIO

- 3RD Finger Record Pool
  210 Walden Glen Cir, Cincinnati, OH 45321
  P) 513-851-8260 F) 513-851-1484
  Ams_star@msn.com

- Central Ohio Record Pool
  3766 Patricia Drive Columbus, OH 43220
  P) 614-442-3396

Mail@ohiopool.com

- Midwestern Dance Association
  16004 Broadway Ave #502, Maple Heights, OH 44137
  P) 216-662-3662 F) 216-662-4977

OKLAHOMA

- Infinity Machine Record Pool
  8605 Muzany LN, Oklahoma City, OK 73135
  P) 405-739-0549

- Oklahoma Record Pool
  2008 N.W. 19th St, Oklahoma City, OK 73106
  P) 405-258-0550 F) 404-258-0660
  okrecpool@aol.com

PENNSYLVANIA

- Jazsays Record Pool
  834 Esteila Ave. #3, Pittsburgh, PA 15210
  P) 412-241-4565 F) 412-243-0651

- Keystone Spinners Record Pool
  361 Bradford Lane, Lansdale, PA 19446
  P) 215-699-2466 F) 215-699-6448
  www.keystonespinners.com
  keystonspinners@attglobal.net

- Needle Wreck Record Pool
  446 Weilsley Rd, Philadelphia, PA 19119
  P) 215-753-1907 F) 215-753-9095
  nedlwrek@vcsn.com

- No Frills
  3654 Daniel Drive .W., Homestead, PA 15120
  P) 412-363-2670 F) 214-363-8887

- Pennpool

1322 Tweed Ave., Allentown, PA 18103
P) 610-797-7552

- Philadelphia Discmasters
  1 Brown St. (Gotham NC), Philadelphia, PA19123
  P) 215-928-9319 F) 215-5921983

- Pittsburgh Disc Jockey Association
  2857 Castleview Drive, Pittsburgh, PA 15227
  P) 412-885-1472 F) 412-885-4027
  PDJA60@aol.com

- Pittsburgh's BPM Record Pool
  134 Watkins Ave., Wilmerding, PA 15148
  P) 412-829-8059 F) 412-829-8059
  tkbmrp@juno.com

- S.J. All-Star Record Pool
  421 N. 7th, Suite 608, Philadelphia, PA 19123
  SJALLSTARPOOL@aol.com

- Top 15 Record Pool
  2960 Wilson School Lane Sinking Spring, PA 19608
  P) 610-670-0552 F) 610-670-0552
  BobbyGthang@msn.com

PUERTO RICO

- Puerto Rico Music Pool
  1020 Corazonez Ave., Mayaguez, PR 00680
  P) 787-647-0216 F) 787-831-6112
  prmusicpool@rocketmail.com

RHODE ISLAND

- Rhode Island D.J
  38 Bainbridge Ave., Providence, RI 02909
  P) 401-272-7838

SOUTH CAROLINA

- Columbia Record Pool
  Contact: Paul Davis
  PMB 228 6169 Saint Andrews Rd, Columbia, SC 29212
  P) 803-561-0393
  crpool@aol.com

- First Break Record
  275 Macy St. Sumter, SC 29153
  P) 803-773-9688 F) 803-773-9688
  1stbreak@gte.net

- South Carolina Record Pool
  100 Stamford Bridge Rd., Columbia, SC 29212
  P) 803-781-4306 F) 803-781-7346
  SCRECORDPOOL@aol.com

- The Carolina Record and CD Pool
  P.O. Box 280187, Columbia, SC 29228
  P) 803-955-2222 P) 888-4-LIFE-18
  www.entertainment4life.com

TEXAS

- A.T.O.M. Record Pool
  23002 Bay Leaf Dr. Spring, TX 77373
  P) 281-350-4074 F) 413-383-3062
  mobetter@iname.com

- Mix Wiz Disc Jockey Association
  4612 Kingsbury St, Houston, TX 77021
  P) 713-748-7060 F) 713-748-1334
  www.mixwizdj.com
  mixwiz@swbell.net

- North Texas Dance Association
  6162 E. Mockingbird LN, Suite# 114, Dallas, TX 75214
  P) 214-826-6832 F) 214-821-6832

director@ntxda.com

- S and S Record Pool
  1006 Outpost Cove, Round Rock, TX 78664
  P) 512-246-8228 F) 512-246-8212

VIRGINA

- Breaking Da Hit Record Pool
  1808 Glen Thorne Rd. Richmond, VA 23222
  P) 804-321-1001 F) 804-321-5757
  Jrs20009@netscape.net

WASHINGTON

- Northwester Dance music Association
  10522 Lake City Way NE Suite # C204
  Seattle, WA 98125
  P) 206-440-9780 F) 206-440-9775
  info@nwdma.org

WASHINGTON D.C.

- Our Mid Atlantic Pool
  1714 Swann St. N.W, Washington D.C 20009
  P) 202-483-8880 F) 202-328-0090
  OMAPinDC@aol.com

- Street Tech Record Pool
  2500 Wisconsin Ave, NW# 425, Washington, DC 20007
  P) 202-463-0110 F) 202-338-0214

WISCONSIN

- Another Level Record Pool
  4405 N 36th, Milwaukee, WI 53209
  P) 414-871-0736 F) 414-871-0748
  neal@mailcity.com

- Wisconsin Music Pool
  833 Ocean Rd., Madison, WI 53717
  P) 608-239-9082 F) 608-257-5128
  sthomas@itis.com

TALENT
SHOWS

The Truth about Talent Shows & Open Mics

The truth about talent shows and open-mics is most artists and the local music community don't benefit from them. The reason is a bit more complex than the music business being plagued by industry sharks taking advantage of the unknowing. The truth is talent shows and open-mics often don't benefit the artists and the local music community because by default they are not designed to.

My goal throughout this section is to give details that will empower everyone involved in the talent showcase and open-mic experience with information that will allow these events to begin to benefit the artist and the local music community. In addition, my goal is to have artists, producers, managers, talent showcase organizers and other music business professional's upgrade their thinking and revise how they work together during a showcase or open mic so that the live performance opportunity is beneficial for them and fans alike.

In this section I intend on accomplishing a few goals. First, you should begin to rethink the talent showcase and open-mic experience. Second, through the Q&A below I hope to share how the events may be a mutually beneficial arrangement for everyone involved including music fans, performing artists, the local music community, club owners and the talent show organizers. Third, I give specific details on how precision planning and execution will help everyone involved benefit from the talent showcase and open mic experience.

What should an artist expect from an open-mic?

Repeatedly, I hear artists complaining that the talent show or open-mic was not what they expected or that there weren't enough people there. My response is: "What did you expect to happen from the show and how many people did you invite to see you perform?" The artist's answer has become fairly repetitive. Normally, they say they were not sure what to expect and that they did not invite anyone to see them perform. Well perhaps the show is not what they expected because they did not know what to expect. More importantly, they did not have clearly identifiable written goals that would allow them to measure the success of the event. For instance, one goal would be to distribute flyers to everyone in attendance, while another would be to get as many email addresses as possible. Many artists don't take every performance serious enough. While you should have fun as you perform your music, also know that if you want to play in the major leagues it is best to perform as such. You get out of a talent show what you put into it.

Artists should expect for the show not to start on time, for the sound to be messed up, for there to be disorganization and for others to be extremely unprofessional. Doing so will allow you to mentally prepare for things to go wrong and how you should deal with them when they do. This will set you apart from the other performers and help present you as the professional that you are. Sometimes the show will go on without any problems, but this is rare and should not be expected. Never complain about the stage, the lighting, the sound and so forth while at the show. Simply do what it takes to correct them and if you can't- entertain your audience and perform. Remember your audience understands if something is not right, but what they don't want to hear is an artist on stage complaining. If you have to perform without music do so! Make a joke, get the crowd involved, and perform. If your mic cuts off in the middle of your performance, keep going, it probably will come back on.

Should an artist perform at a talent show?

Despite what some aspiring artist and music industry professionals believe, recording artist don't make the bulk of their money from having their music sold. Rather they get paid from endorsement deals, merchandising sales and playing live. I don't know any artist who has gotten some sort of deal in the business who has not performed at an open-mic or talent show at some point. It really is about, perfecting your craft, paying your dues and building a loyal fan base that will help push you through your journey of success.

Performing live is where artist get to see how well their music and image connects with new and existing supporters. If an artist can perform in front of one person they can perform in front of ten, one hundred, a thousand and so forth. Gigging is a much different experience than studio recording. While recording in the studio you have the luxury of replaying a part or doing your vocals over again should you need to. However, when playing live you have got to deal with every hick up that might come your way. Performing at a talent show or open-mic is a must do for any aspiring artist, singer, rapper, musician, band or group.

Difference between a talent show & open-mic

Talent show performers are screened, practice regularly and normally are ready to play in the Major Leagues. Talent shows may have professionals from record companies, labels and other industry executives seeking hot new talent. In addition, talent shows generally have auditions or are very selective about the performers in its shows. Many of the artists performing in talent shows tend to have either a local or regional following. In addition, while some talent shows may be "regularly scheduled" or "routinely scheduled", they may not be as frequent as open-mics. For instance, On Stage Live Revue, a showcase held by Bar Red Entertainment, takes place six times a year in Atlanta.

Open-mics generally have no real screening process. In fact open-mics are often used by local acts to perform new material in front of their peers. Musicians or performers of the same style music often attend open-mics. Open-mics tend to be frequently regularly scheduled events. For instance, an open-mic might be held once a week or twice a month at the same venue. Generally, there is a sign-up period and as long as you get there by the specified time you will be put on the list to perform. Open-mics are held for singers, rappers, bands, poets and comedians. Sometimes one open-mic will be open to all genres of talent while others focus on a particular type or style of music.

Can I get signed from playing at an open mic?

Anything is possible by highly unlikely. An open mic merely acts as a conduit for showcasing aspiring artist. However, it cannot be overstated that artists should view their live performance experience as yet another stepping stone in building their career as a recording and performing artist. When an A&R rep attends a showcase they are normally there by request to see a particular band or group perform. Often they have heard of the group before and possibly even are seeking to sign them. Throughout the Atlanta Music Industry Connection Book I give details about how an aspiring artist, band or group should go about branding, marketing and promoting themselves and how important that is. This information is extremely important as it is what typically gets the attention of talent scouts and label A&R.

This, of course, is in addition to having a fantastic sound, star quality and a high level of professionalism.

Given that you have the opportunity to meet an A&R while at a talent show, attempt not to over talk yourself. Don't over hype your band or group saying you are the next so and so and that you sound better than the artist currently receiving heavy rotation on commercial radio. After all, the artist you're mentioning might be a personal friend of the A&R you are talking to. The A&R may have been very instrumental in getting that artist signed to the label. The music industry is a small circle of people. It would be a shame if you were unable to get into the circle because of something you said while attempting to promote your group.

When approaching the A&R, introduce yourself and ask them for advice for an aspiring artist, tips for success or books that may help you further your music career. The point here is to show your interest in the business at large. This may set you apart from other artist who too think they are the next big commercial success the A&R should help sign. You will want to ask for a business card and invite them to your next performance. **This part is extremely important: tell them that you will not abuse their contact information nor send them music without their permission**. Often industry types will say, "Oh, hey, I don't have any cards right now, may I have one of yours?" I have seen it happen many times before. The funny thing is the person will turn right around and hand their card to someone else. If this happens to you, don't take personal offense. The person may only have a few cards left and came with the intention of giving them to someone else or they don't want to receive more demos, cards and emails than they already get. Put yourself in their shoes. A&R's have a number of artists who want to submit demos in an effort to get signed. Many times these artists have not taking the steps to perfect their craft, improve their stage presence and image nor are they actively branding, marketing and promoting themselves. For the A&R, it becomes a waste of time and energy.

Remember a talent show merely acts as a conduit for showcasing aspiring artists, bands and groups. However, it cannot be overstated that artists should view their live performance experiences as yet another stepping stone in building their career as a recording and performing artist. Remember, A&R reps usually attend a showcase because they are invited to see a particular artist or group. Perhaps at your next gig the A&R will be there to see you perform.

How much networking takes place during an open-mic?

Before attending a talent show or open-mic, I go with the intent on distributing as many books, business cards and flyers as possible. In addition, I seek to get email addresses from everyone there. For me networking is fantastic at talent shows and open-mics. However, I tend to have very specific measurable goals. Also I have the tools necessary to help make my networking experience a blast. Artist often come to these events with no promotional CDs, no business cards, no flyers and no ink pens -expecting to benefit from the potential networking opportunity. Other industry folks will also be ill prepared and might ask me to remember their email address. It has been my experience that you typically get more out of someone when you are of service to them versus asking them to service you. Essentially, you would want to write down your contact information if you have run out of business cards or other promotional material.

The amount of networking that takes place during a talent showcase or open-mic varies based on who you ask. To ensure you increase your opportunity, set measurable goals and bring the tools necessary to help you achieve those goals. Bring promotional CDs, business cards, flyers, ink pens and so forth. In the Atlanta Music Industry

Connection and Los Angeles Music Industry Connection Books I give business names, physical mailing addresses, emails, websites, phone and fax numbers to CD manufacturers and printing companies in those areas. To get details on other books and their audio components visit www.mt101.com.

Why should a producer attend a talent show?

As an aspiring music producer, you are seeking to have your music placed on future releases and to sell your tracks. By attending talent shows you position yourself to network with artists who may have a major label deal pending, artists who are selling significant units signed to an independent label and other industry professionals. Through your networking efforts you should create and cultivate relationships that will afford you the opportunities to produce music for artist who have the potential to become break out artists.

As a producer you will want to have business cards, flyers and CDs sampling some of your work. I would put no more than three to five tracks on a CD. My rational is that if your music is hot enough it will warrant a call back. Remember to include as many contact details on your CD and as an audio track as possible. This will ensure that if someone wants to contact you about work, it will be easy to do so. Your contact details should include your name, company name, phone number, email and website addresses.

Why should a manager attend an open-mic?

There are several reasons why a manager should attend a talent show or open-mic. First, the manager may attend these events in search of new talent. While it's possible to find an artist at these events, a manager is generally seeking ,a more polished environment in which to discover new talent. The manager is generally seeking to get a better look and feel of a recording and performing artist, band or group at a talent show or open- mic. Second, the manager may want to know what new trends, sounds and styles of music are on the rise. Artist often use open-mics as testing ground for new material. Third, the manager may seek to network with other music business professionals. Open-mics typically bring local movers and shakers out especially in smaller markets. By attending open-mics a manager will be able to keep their thumb on the pulse of the independent scene and find out what new artist may be on the verge of the break out. For instance, by talking to other professionals a manager may determine what artist has a loyal following or fan base. Last, the goal of attending talent shows or open-mics may be to determine if the show is right for the managers' artists to perform in sometime in the future. Some managers want their artist to get on stage every chance they get, while others are very particular about where their artist is seen performing. Both ways can work. As long as the plan is thought out and in writing, it will be easier to implement.

Should I sell my music at a talent show?

In today's music business environment artist should consider themselves as a business and not merely artists. Every business has to sell a product or service. A recording artist who is also a business is at an advantage because they can sell both. The product would be any medium on which the music may be played or stored. For instance, a compact disc would be the physical product. In addition, the artist could sale their merchandise, such as t-shirts, hats and posters with their name and logo on them. Make sure you give yourself optimum protection under the letter of the law by properly trademarking your logo. You may do it yourself or hire an entertainment attorney to do it for you. Contacts for entertainment attorneys and details about trademarking may be found in both the Atlanta Music Industry Connection and Los Angeles Music Industry Connection Books. In addition to selling product, bands may sell their service as performing artists. Essentially, that is what happens when a band is paid to perform live: they are selling their services.

I would like to see more artist selling their music and merchandise at talent shows and open-mics. There are music fans that want to be on the cutting edge of new music and buying independent releases at live performances is one way for them to achieve their goal. Absolutely, artist, bands, singers, rappers and musicians should sell their music whenever they perform. Remember to keep track of how many CDs and shirts you sold, when you sold them and at what price. This will help you when it is time to do taxes, to evaluate how and where you tend to sell the most of your product and to demonstrate to potential investors the value of your growing enterprise.

How do you get the industry to attend talent shows?

First, the talent performing should be of star quality. The artist should be professional and look and sound as though they are ready for the Big Leagues. As the talent show or open mic gains credibility for having polished talent, industry executives and talent scouts will come out. Once they see, hear and network with polished talent they will share the information with other music industry professionals. Before you know it more and more A&R, DJs and so forth will be attending these events. When more people will attend these events, it increases the networking opportunity for everyone.

The talent show and open-mic organizers and the artists performing must all do their part in inviting music industry professionals to the events. The show organizers will want to email, fax, snail mail and call the executives hyping the show and invite them to view the polished talent. Likewise, the artists will need to invite local movers and shakers such as entertainment and music magazine editors, music retail store managers and owners, DJs, record pool directors, club owners and managers. A list of these various professionals may be found in the Atlanta Music Industry Connection and Los Angeles Music Industry Connection Books.

Why do some talent shows charge to perform?

Venue space such as the club, flyers, gas, websites and email blast to promote, sound engineer, DJ and so forth are all expenses that may be incurred by talent show and open-mic organizers. All this and there is no guarantee that anyone will pay to see the acts perform. By charging either an audition fee or fee to perform, organizers of talent shows and open-mics reduce their costs. In addition, it helps to screen out talent that may not be serious about their careers.

Because there are unscrupulous individuals organizing these shows, I am going to set some parameters for clarity. First, an audition is just that- an audition. It does not guarantee that you will perform in the show. Many organizers charge some administration-processing fee for auditioning. This is not necessarily a bad thing, as long as the artist clearly understands that they are auditioning with the potential to perform in the show, yet it is not promised. This information should be plainly stated in writing and be made available for every artist seeking to audition. In addition, if the fee to audition is relatively high, the event organizers may consider allowing all talent to audition for free. This would increase the attendance. Second, some talent shows allow just about anyone to perform as long as they pay their money to get on stage. This is not necessarily a bad thing as long as the artist understands the amount of time they have to perform, how many people can be on stage while they perform, the time they need to be at the venue and the time they can expect to perform.

While I am not in total opposition to artist paying to perform, I do think artist should be given ways to generate money from their performance on the back end if they are not being paid upfront. For instance, they should be able to sell tickets and receive monies from every ticket that they sell. In addition, artist should be encouraged to sell their music at the shows. While all venues may not be conducive for doing so, it would be fantastic if the artist had a section of the club where they could set up tables to sell their music and merchandise.

Should I pay to perform?

Paying to perform is purely an artist's decision, much of which is based on ego and the prestige of the show. Some artists feel that they should be paid to perform versus paying to perform. At the end of the day, it boils down to the perception and reality of your value in the market place. If you have a significant following, radio or video airplay and, more importantly, are currently being sought after by booking agents, then perhaps you would not need to pay to perform. However, if you are still building your fan base, seeking commercial radio and video airplay and negotiating terms with booking agents, you may want to pay to perform. If you write realistic measurable goals, increase your exposure and create opportunities to generate money- every performance will be a success, some of which you may pay to perform.

Treating local talent shows like mini concerts.

While artist should always respect the mic, the stage and the time allotted by talent show and open-mic organizers, they should perform professionally as though it was their major concert. In fact, bands, artists, groups and performers should treat every performance as though it where their mini concert. This is accomplished by first envisioning yourself before, during and after getting on stage. You must be able to mentally see yourself performing in front of thousands of people. Then you must rehearse to perfection as though your life depended on it. Once you have done that, then you can truly begin practicing for your live performance, mentally and physically preparing to give your audience an experience they will never forget.

Something I know to be true is that a super star artist (no matter what genre of music) will generally always get and retain the respect and attention of their audience. While attending a talent show a young man performed a country song. Initially, he appeared a bit out of his element as most of the audience anticipated seeing Hip Hop and R&B artists perform that evening. The young man was dressed the part, had dancers, stage presence, a rehearsed routine, plenty of energy and his music was of excellent sound quality. To most people's or attendee's surprise, he turned the show out, gained and retained the respect of his audience. In addition, he was prepared and viewed his performance that evening as his mini concert. You see in the back of the club he had a set up where he signed autographs, sold CDs, collected email addresses and greeted everyone he could even if they did not see his performance. Remember to take every performance seriously and give your audience a memorable experience as though they paid high-ticket prices to see you perform.

Do A&R really look for new acts at open-mics?

More so than going to a showcase or open-mic to seek new talent, A&R reps at major record companies will attend these events because they have been invited to come or because they have an interest in a particular band, group or artist- meaning someone they are already considering signing. However, what you do have a lot of are independent A&R reps and scouts regularly attending talent shows and open-mics.

Independent A&R reps typically acts as a private contractors or free agents with no allegiance to any particular record company. They may have relationships with a number of companies and seek to pair artists with companies. These independent A&R reps normally get a commission when the artist is signed or when a deal is finalized. More independent A&R reps are seeking not just to get artist signed, but also to create revenue generating potential and exposure opportunities for artists. For example, some of these reps have relationships with video game or film production companies that are always seeking new music. By giving the artist access to these companies, it increases their revenue earning potential and exposure opportunities.

While scouts serve a similar function as an A&R, they tend to be on the front lines and usually are the ones regularly attending talent showcases and open-mics seeking new talent. Talent scouts often work for an A&R, whether at a label or as independent company. Some of the differences between an A&R rep and a talent scout are historically A&R rep's developed and signed star talent, whereas talent scouts where merely the eyes and ears of new talent. In addition, talent scouts typically get paid a lot less money than A&R reps. Talent scouts normally have no real authority as to who gets signed to a label and who doesn't.

SHADY SHOWCASES

I was getting out of my car preparing to go in an open-mic when Haziq said, "JaWar, talk to this artist. He is a bit frustrated with Atlanta's Open-mic & Talent Showcase Scene." I introduced myself as JaWar, author of the fastest selling music business book in Atlanta, *the Atlanta Music Industry Connection: Resources for Artists, Producers and Managers*. The artist said he was from Macon, Georgia and that the only people that were in the open-mic were rappers- no A&R or industry people that could help his career. I asked him what he expected of the open-mic. He said he thought label reps and other music business people would be there. He shared how all the open-mics are the same, they charge you money to perform and you don't get anything out of it. I asked him if he would like to briefly look through the Atlanta Music Industry Connection Book. He said "Sure, why not?!" During this time I introduced him to Hugh. Hugh is a talent showcase organizer and normally does shows outside of the metropolitan area (smart move). Typically he gets anywhere from 100 to 300 people at his shows.

Hugh asked the artist for a promotional CD. The artist replied, "I don't have any promotional CDs." I asked the artists how much does the CD cost, he replied "I don't have any for sell." "HOLD ON" I said, "There is part of the problem; You don't have any tangible product." The artist said, "Wait a minute- listen to this," then he started rapping. Hmmmmmmm, after he stopped I said "What was that?" He said "I got skills." "Yes," I replied, "but Hugh can't take your skills with him, I can't give your skills to a radio programmer, DJ, music magazine editor or any other music business professional. More importantly your skills can't be sold in that form. This is Atlanta" I told him, "everyone raps or knows someone that raps around here. What you did was not special." I said. I asked the artist if he had a business card or flyer with his email address on it, as I would like to add him to the MIC-Music Industry Connection E-Magazine, he said no.

"Perhaps you are frustrated with the Atlanta's Open-Mic Scene because you don't have a practical written plan and the necessary tools to execute that plan. Perhaps you have unrealistic expectations of performing live," I said. "The Atlanta Music Industry Connection & Los Angeles Music Industry Connection Books and my audio book, 18 Most FAQ's about the Music Biz will help you have a better over-standing of how the industry works. More importantly, you may use it as a guide to help you move your career forward faster. Would you like to get a copy of either the book or audio book?" He said "I'm a little short right now."

Unfortunately, I have similar experiences with artist's from different genres of music week in and week out around the country. I have identified a few reasons why artists don't succeed and often become frustrated with the process of building a profitable, lasting music career. Many artists have not upgraded their thinking to be more optimistic and positive. They often miss windows of opportunities by not doing so. Most artists don't have a written plan or a road map to guide their careers. They are not willing to sacrifice to achieve their goals and realize their potential. Artists often think they have MADE IT and have little work ethic. For instance, they aren't willing to distribute flyers and perform relentlessly week in and week out but they rarely invite the industry to their live performances. The industry would include music retail store owners/managers, DJs, music and entertainment writers, music publicists, online music sites and so forth. Finally, artists simply have not recorded those hot songs; you know the undeniable hits, the ones that you immediately embrace.

If you are an artist, independent label, production or management company, entertainment law firm, publicist or other music business professional and need to create and implement a strategic and marketing plan, you will want to get a book under the Music Industry Connection Book Series. After reading the book I may better assist you in achieving your goals and realize your potential during a one-on-one consultation. For details call 800-963-0949 or email questions@mt101.com

GET CASH CAMPAIGN FOR THE MUSIC INDUSTRY

Every music industry conference, talent show, open-mic and networking event should be used to GET CASH for the MUSIC INDUSTRY. Here is how it works; every music industry professional must first identify their target market. Artist markets typically are people who buy music, not industry professionals who receive music for free. Talent showcase and open-mic organizers markets are typically artists, musicians, singers, rappers, bands and their music fans. Music & Entertainment magazine's markets are readers and advertisers. Producer's markets typically are artists, songwriters and labels. An entertainment attorneys market is everyone in the industry that needs consulting, contract negotiating, drafting and courtroom representation (I should have gone to law school). Other professionals include managers, engineers, promoters, photographers, graphic artists and consultants, DJs, singers, songwriters, music publishers, publicists, web-designers, CD manufacturers and record pools; all of which may benefit from increased exposure during a talent showcase, open-mic or music conference.

Serious recording and performing artist should be able to get 10 to 20 people to come see them perform. Given that ten artist perform in a particular show something mathematical begins to occur. The show now has anywhere from 100 to 200 paying music fans.

Lets consider for a moment that ten artists were paying $50 to perform in a talent show or open-mic and have the ability to sell their music & merchandise during the event. Selling music would include the physical and digital formats most widely accepted by the buying public. Merchandise would include t-shirts, tank tops, hats and so forth. For $50 the artist would receive a 3 to 5 minute performance slot and a vending table in a high foot trafficked area where they could openly sell their music & merchandise. Artist would get their investment back after selling 5 CDs at $10 each (5/CDs X $10= $50) or selling 10 CDs at $5 each (10/CDs X $5=$50). The beauty is that because nine other artists each brought 10 to 20 fans, there are potentially 90 to 180 new fans that the artist has access to. Artists who are serious about their craft and a career in the business should be able to get 10 to 20 paying fans at $5 each to see them perform. To be a successful independent touring artist, you will need to be able to draw at least a few hundred fans per show. As you do, club promoters can justify paying you to perform. You should also sell your band's merchandise constantly, giving you an additional revenue stream. Remember you can sell CDs, shirts, hats, posters and the like. Given that the merchandise will have your groups name and logo on them, you are generating cash while promoting yourself at the same time. That's fantastic! It would be wise to ask supporters to join your email list. By including people in your list you can inform them of future gigs, new releases and autograph signings.

Cities like Atlanta, Los Angeles, Nashville and New York have well over ten talent show and open-mic organizers. These organizers all seek polished talent and their fans at the events they organize. One of the ways to locate talent is to go where the talent is performing. What if talent showcase and open-mic organizers extended a warm invitation to other event organizers by allowing them to set up a vending table for $25 to $35? This would build the local music scene, increase networking opportunities and boost revenue for all the event organizers. Let's do the math. At $25 X 10/organizers = $250 ($25 X 10 = $250) or $35 X 10/organizers = $350 ($35 X 10= $350). The vendors should have a sign up sheet so they may contact artists interested in performing in their show. By having event organizers in one venue artists have the ability to learn more about other performance opportunities. They would be given date, time, location and requirements for performing in other events. The artists will appreciate the talent show and open-mic organizer for providing them with this service. You see, I get emails and phone calls from all over the country with performers always asking if I know of any places where they may perform. These artists want to perform in as many venues as possible. Unfortunately, some talent show and open-mic organizers see my idea of allowing other event organizers to vend at their talent show or open-mic as competition instead of a cooperative business environment. The auto industry, fast-food restaurants and clothing stores all benefit from bringing a large number of consumers together in one place at one time. The auto industry does it in the form of an auto mall where several different car manufacturers will have dealerships on the same street. Fast-food restaurants do it by having a food court in the mall. Clothing stores do it by having a number of different stores in a mall. Talent showcase and open-mic organizers should begin to create opportunities for everyone at the event. By doing so, they automatically increase their earning potential and longevity in the industry. They also ensure that the local music scene continues to flourish. At the end of the day this all will help increase the GET CASH CAMPAIGN for the MUSIC INDUSTRY.

The artist has a responsibility of getting 10 to 20 fans to each of their shows. This should not be difficult given that they follow the steps found in the Atlanta Music Industry Connection & the Los Angeles Music Industry Connection Books. The talent show or open-mic organizer has a responsibility of screening polished talent and ensuring that the event is a great one. They also are commissioned with properly promoting the event by sending emails, faxes and distributing flyers to other music business professionals in an effort to get them to come to the show. The show should start on time, the sound should be as perfect as possible, the lighting should be set for the event and the staff should be professional and courteous. Fans have a responsibility of supporting their favorite artist by paying to see them perform and buying their CDs and merchandise at the event.

Record company A&R, music magazines, DJs, publicists, entertainment attorneys and so forth want to see polished talent perform. They also want to see that the talent understands the business and that they are actively promoting themselves selling product and merchandise while building a loyal fan base. Everyone gets excited about a fantastic band or performer that is creating opportunities for them and others. As a recurring talent showcase or open-mic continues to present polished performers music, industry decision-makers will attend the event regularly. Word-of-mouth marketing and promotions will begin to take shape and others will want to come to the talent show so they to can increase their contacts through networking and benefit from the GET CASH CAMPAIGN for the MUSIC INDUSTRY.

The talent showcase or open-mic organizer would generate the following revenue from this scenario. Twenty fans times ten performers equals two hundred fans or (20 X 10 = 200).

200 fans X $5	**= $1,000**
10/artists X $50	**= $ 500**
10/organizers X $25	**= $ 250**
Gross Revenue/Show	**= $1,750**

This plan is great, but what if you were to have a weekly event. You could generate seven thousand dollars a month ($1,750 X 4 = $7,000). This could be achieved given that the market is large enough to support such an effort. I think it would really work if you were to give showcases or open-mics in different styles of music. Some styles of music would include Rock, Hip Hop, Country, Jazz, Gospel, Pop, Alternative, R&B, Metal, Punk, Blues and so forth. As an organizer you will want to bring in different media sponsors to help you brand, market and promote your events. Music and entertainment magazines, music groups and websites, commercial, college and Internet radio stations, public access and cable television are all possible media sponsors. As you bring on media sponsors your alliances begin to grow and you position yourself to be a major player in the local music scene. Overtime your event will start to include artists from around the region and country. Inevitably, you become the "go to" person. Other professionals will seek you out not just because you have a dynamic talent showcase or open-mic, but because you have built a solid brand and industry contacts. Your ideas become valued in the business. People will begin looking toward you to find and develop talent and to make big things happen in the market. This and many other things are achieved when you open your mind and actions to helping others.

In order for the GET CASH CAMPAIGN for the MUSIC INDUSTRY to work using the talent show and open-mic as a viable business model, everyone must do their part. Because I have shared details on how the talent showcase and open-mic organizer could generate thousands of dollars monthly, given that the GET CASH CAMPAIGN for the MUSIC INDUSTRY is implemented, **I ask that you purchase a copy of the Atlanta Music Industry Connection Book and grant me access to your music industry conference, networking event, talent show or open-mic, so I may witness others accomplishing their goals and so the Music Industry Connection Book Series may be distributed**. As this happens, more people get involved in the process. The system begins to take form or take shape, the local music market grows and various industry professionals have the opportunity to increase their cash flow from one event. The possibilities are monumental. I guarantee that if everyone does their part, great things will come, things that I have not yet mentioned, but that are destined. The Atlanta Music Industry Connection Book & the Los Angeles Music Industry Connection Books have hundreds of company names, physical mailing addresses, phone & fax numbers, email and website addresses to recording studios, mastering engineers, retail stores, music distributors, entertainment attorneys, managers, photographers, music conferences, record pools, radio stations and so forth. The books also give details on **How to Market Your Independent Release & How to Use Record Pools to Test-Market Your Next Hit** and are filled with additional articles, essays and needed resources to assist everybody mentioned in achieving the GET CASH CAMPAIGN for the MUSIC INDUSTRY. The Atlanta Music Industry Connection & the Los Angeles Music Industry Connection Books may be ordered in bulk by talent showcase and open-mic organizers seeking to sell books at their events or to include them in the registration package for artists who perform in their shows. **Call 800-963-0949 or 678-887-4656 for details.**

Single book sales may be placed at www.mt101.com, by visiting your local music or bookstore or by completing the order form at the end of this book.

CREATING WEALTH

Whether you earn an additional $5,000 or $5,000,000 a year from the business of music, remember to always put a percentage of your earnings (money that you make) aside, preferably in a tax-sheltered account and invest your money in businesses that have nothing to do with the music industry. This is called diversification of your assets (money). In addition, **you want to always pay yourself first**, spend less money than you earn, carry little to no consumer debt and keep accurate and complete records of the money you earn and spend. This will increase your chances for long-term wealth creation and retention. **Educate yourself about business and money; after all if you don't mind your business and money, someone else will.** To ensure you advance your own learning on saving, investing and creating wealth, I have listed a few terms below that you should know.

401(k)
Annuities
Assets
Asset Allocation
Bonds
- Corporate
- Convertible
- Government
CD-Certificate of Deposit
Checking Account
Compounding Interest
Debt to Income Ratio
Diversification
Dollar-Cost Averaging
Earnings
Equity
Financial Freedom
Index Funds
Inflation
Investment Portfolio

IRA-Individual Retirement Account
Keoghs
Market Index
Money-Market Accounts
Money Market Mutual Funds
NAV (Net Asset Value)
No-Load Mutual Funds
Passive Income
Prospectus
Real Estate
Residual Income
ROI (Return on Investment)
Roth-IRA, SEP-IRA, Simple-IRA
Savings Account
Stocks
Tax Sheltered Accounts
Treasury Bills

Educate yourself about investing and seek the advice of professionals who may help you verify your information. Some professionals include: an accountant, tax advisor, C.P.A. (Certified Public Accountant), financial planner, business manager and so forth. These professionals should be as key to your team as your manager, entertainment attorney, booking agent or publicists.

Publications that may help you become familiar with saving and investing your money are Black Enterprise, The Wall Street Journal, Kiplinger, Money, Smart Money, Barron's, Investor Business Daily, Financial Times, the Business Section of your local city paper and the Money Section of USA Today. For more information on saving, investing and making your money grow; visit the following websites.

- www.bankrate.com
- www.blackenterprise.com
- www.buyandhold.com
- www.creditinfocenter.com
- www.fool.com
- www.indexfunds.com
- www.investoreducation.org
- www.jumpstartcoalition.org
- www.kiplinger.com
- www.marketwatch.com
- www.mfea.com
- www.money.com
- www.moneyopolis.org
- www.moringstar.com
- www.richdadpoordad.com
- www.rothira.com
- www.smartmoney.com
- www.tiaacref.com
- www.troweprice.com
- www.youdecide.com
- www.vanguard.com

VISUALLY STIMULATING THE WAY YOU'RE PERCEIVED...

DESIGN APART

Urban & Corporate design

album covers
demo cd/mixed tapes
logos
business cards
promotional posters
t-shirts
professional photography
club flyers

404_351+4312 | designashil@yahoo.com

MUSIC BIZ
WORKSHOP
Music Therapy 101
National Music Seminar
mt101.com

**Singers, Rappers, Producers
and Musicians
attend this dynamic seminar
to learn about
the music business & industry.**

Attend workshops on
Legal Issues, Marketing & Promotions
Building Your Business, Radio & Retail, etc.,
and the Interactive Activity *How to Press 1,000
Retail Ready CDs Without Using Your Own Money*
presented by JaWar.

**Go to WWW.MT101.COM for future
Music Therapy 101 dates, times and locations**

Sponsored by:  **KEMETIC
RECORDS**
www.kemetic.com

Audiovascular
Entertainment

For sponsorship and vending opportunities
call 800-963-0949 or www.mt101.com

93

Place A Full Page Ad In

(THE MIC)
MUSIC INDUSTRY CONNECTION BOOK SERIES

contact
800-963-0949 or 678-887-4656
questions@mt101.com

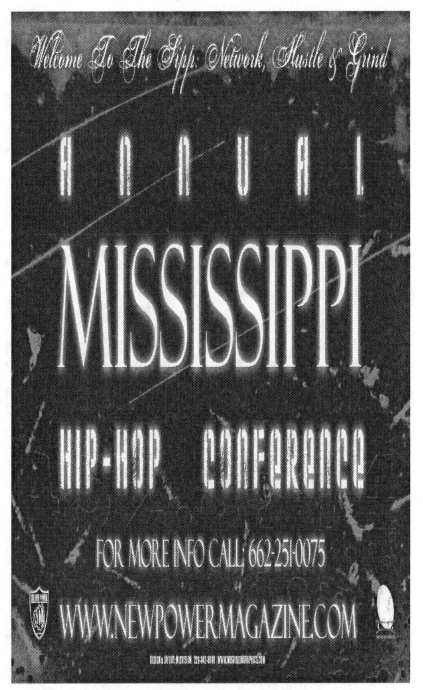

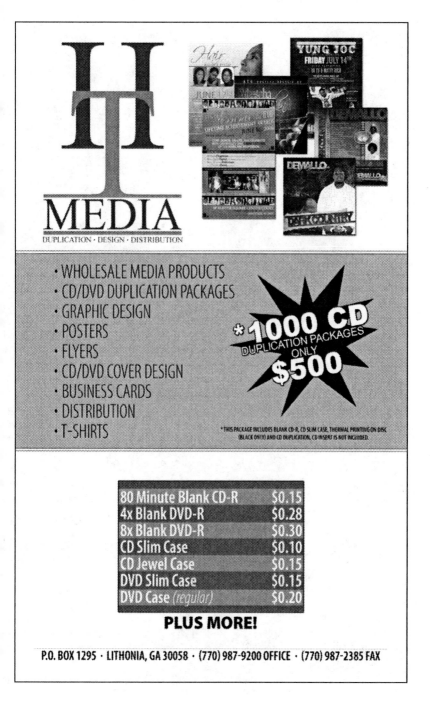

Entertainment Business Support
ATLANTA • GA

Ph. 404.217.0696
email. kfennell@entertainmentbizsupport.com
web. www.entertainmentbizsupport.com

PUBLISH YOUR BOOK

Share Your Story With The World!

Your story is too important to continue collecting dust in the basement, attic or garage. Your story is too important to wait for another publishing house's approval. Your story is too important to wait for the approval of an agent. Your story is too important for you to let fear stop you from achieving your goals and realizing your success.

Do as you were meant to do; take control of your own destiny and fulfill your dreams of becoming a published author. Your book may save a life, inspire another and bring you unparalleled happiness, but only if you take action today!

I am JaWar, author of the fastest selling music business book in Atlanta, the Atlanta Music Industry Connection, Resources for Artists, Producers and Managers. I was making less than $10/hour, working no more than 24 hours a week when the first edition of the Atlanta Music Industry Connection Book was published. As a child, I had a strong speech impediment, I stuttered, which made it very challenging for me to speak in public. Today, I conduct workshops and seminars on the business of music and book publishing. More importantly, I have created a system and step-by-step process that will enable most anyone with passion, drive and undeniable hustle to print and publish their own book. I consult businesses and individuals just like you on how to publish their fiction, non-fiction and technical books. Set-up your consultation today by contacting me either at 800-963-0949 or emailing me at jawar@mt101.com

> Eternal Success,
> JaWar

JAWAR

Chief Visionary Officer of Music Therapy 101, a Music Business Conference and Workshop Series since 1998, has given informative seminars in Atlanta-Georgia, Los Angeles-California, Washington D.C., Charlotte-North Carolina and Louisville-Kentucky. He created the workshop to identify and share vital information in a step-by-step process necessary for success and ultimate longevity in the music biz with aspiring artists and those willing to be involved in the music industry.

In 2002, JaWar created the MIC (Music Industry Connection) one of the few free all Music Business Publications that serves all genres of music. In just over a year the MIC tripled is circulation, doubled its' page count and increased its' subscription base. In 2004 JaWar expanded his publishing efforts and released the Atlanta Music Industry Connection: Resources for Artists, Producers & Managers Book, the most comprehensive directory of Atlanta Music Business Professionals in print. When your event demands practical, relevant, and useful details from an enthusiastic speaker who has legitimately "been there" by releasing the Dark Ages II & Paranormal Activity CDs on his independent record company Kemetic Records consider JaWar; he may be contacted at 800-963-0949, jawar@mt101.com or P.O. Box 52682, Atlanta, GA 30355, USA.

JaWar provides music business consulting services with an emphasis on marketing & promotions, strategic planning and profit increasing to select businesses and individuals seeking to advance their companies goals and objectives. Whether through one-on-one consultation or in a business group setting, JaWar may help your business become more efficient and effective.

MAIL ORDER FORM

Please mail me the following music business items to help me achieve my goals. I have completed the attached order form and will include a money order for my total and mail it payable to:

MUSIC INDUSTRY CONNECTION, LLC
P.O. BOX 52682, Atlanta, GA 30355, USA

Name:	
Company Name:	
Mailing address:	
City:	State: Zip:
Phone:	Fax:
Email:	
Comments:	

www.mt101.com 800-963-0949

Item Description	PRICE Per Item	# of Items	Total
Atlanta Music Industry Connection E-Book	$19.95		
Atlanta Music Industry Connection Book: Resources for-Artists, Producers, Managers	$19.95		
Atlanta Music Industry Connection Book: Resources for ARTIST	$19.95		
Atlanta Music Industry Connection Book: Resources for PRODUCERS	$19.95		
Los Angeles Music Industry Connection: Resources for-Artists, Producers, Managers	$19.95		
Music Industry Connection: The Truth About Record Pools & Music Conferences, Talent Shows & Open-Mics **E-Book**	$19.95		
Music Industry Connection: The Truth About Record Pools & Music Conferences, Talent Shows & Open-Mics Book	$19.95		
How to Press 1,000 Retail Ready CDs Without Using Your Own Money Kit	$149.95		
SUBTOTAL	/////////		
Shipping & Handling Add $6.00			
GA residents add 7% sales tax.			
TOTAL			